MELLO   1

THE

mello
COOKBOOK

SUPPORT YOUR BODY & SOUL

GIANNA CIARAMELLO

You learn a lot about someone when you share a meal together.

ANTHONY BOURDAIN

THE mello COOKBOOK

Just a hungry bunny with a love for plant based
foods who wants to share her recipes with
each & every one of you.

Gianna Ciaramello
Author of The Mello Cookbook

& Rabbit Food

Design & Layout by Gianna Ciaramello
Photographs by Gianna Ciaramello

WHAT IS MELLO?

Transcend your self limiting beliefs and awaken the higher aspects of your being, your heart deserves it. This life that you live is so beautiful. No matter how big or how small, you along with every other being on this planet deserves nothing but love.

Get **Mello**. You have all of the power inside of you to take back your life and embrace all the dreams you have in your heart. Feel empowered through your life, your journey and your choices.

Mello is a culmination of all the things that make me who I am. A movement, a rise of breath, a vital force and a stance to be all that you are and all that you are yet to be. **Mello** is my approach to processing the negative elements of life and finding the best way to approach any form of hostility. Have a **Mello** heart and a vibrant soul. Be calm, stay grounded, be present and breathe. Your breath is your life force, an element of your life that you can master.

Mastering your life force, or breath, creates opportunity to reignite with true presence—the key to happiness.

Eliminate the negative mind, worry, anxiousness, as well as any and all of the factors that prevent you from experiencing true bliss. Let it go, because you are in control. Rise, from instinctual to elevated and be all that you wish to be. You cannot extend love by emitting hate. I choose to share experiences, food, opportunities, love and emotion—in the least intimidating way. My motivation is to serve and to inspire you to always continue making a difference in this world. My approach is **Mello**.

gianna ciaramello

FEATURED FOODIES

Julie Simone *Pgs 94 & 95*

Passionate animal advocate and dog Mom with a taste for anything spicy.

Instagram: @kindheartrebel

Mary Mirelez *Pgs 162 & 163*

Mary is a gluten-free home cook, recipe developer, food photographer, creator of the food blog sunshineandseasalt.com, and healthy eating advocate living in Central Texas.

W: sunshineandseasalt.com

Instagram: @sunshineandseasalt

Sam Pickthall *Pgs 74, 75, 186 & 187*

Hi I'm Sam and I created Wholesome Patisserie to share with you my love of deliciously good healthy food, including heavenly sweet treats and vibrant savory meals!

W: wholesomepatisserie.com

Instagram: @wholesomepatisserie

Tawnya Brown *Pgs 182 & 183*

Tawnya is a student who works part time in a coffee shop Her hobbies include cooking, walking at the beach, and spending time with her family.

Instagram: @veganalimon

Monica Bozelle *Pgs 80 & 81*

Monica is a vegan foodie that enjoys spending time in the kitchen creating healthy delicious meals. She is a lover of people, animals & the outdoors and is working on maintaining a balanced lifestyle.

Instagram: @veggieslovepeace

Rebecca Doudak *Pgs 218 & 219*

Rebecca is a NYC native who enjoys exploring creativity in every form. She is passionate about encouraging people to be their true selves, physical fitness, and spreading practical veganism and down-to-earth environmentalism.

Instagram: @veganbodegacat

FEATURED FOODIES

Kemal *Pgs 144 & 145*

An artist, in many mediums

W: therusticvegan.com

Instagram: @rustic.vegan

Magdalena Nickl *Pgs 70, 71, 166 & 167*

Magdalena is a 16 year old vegan from Germany trying to make the world a better place. She believes that we each have an impact on this world and any positive change is still working towards a greater good. Magdalena enjoys drawing, playing the accordion and cooking!

Instagram: @magdalenas_blog

Michelle Gerrard-Marriott *Pgs 184 & 185*

Michelle Gerrard-Marriott is a Vegan Recipe Developer and Freelance Writer. She is a lover of travel and experiencing everything the world has to offer. Michelle is an activist for change and lover of the environment.

W: *the-vibrant-kitchen.com*

Instagram: @thevibrantkitchen

Christina Kee *Pgs 198 & 199*

Christina Kee is a mom to three with Rheumatoid Arthritis and she is passionate about all things health and wellness.
Instagram: @be_chronically_well

Jean Charite *Pgs 202, 203, 204 & 205*

Jean Charite is known on social media as TheBasicVegan. He is an amazing videographer, content creator and passionate vegan foodist.

Instagram: @TheBasicVegan

Marie-Kristin Wasler *Pgs 172, 173, 208 & 209*

Marie is a full-time social media manager by day and a foodie by night (and any other second I'm not working). She has been vegan since this year and feels that choosing this lifestyle was the best decision ever.

Instagram: @pinkfoodieee

CONTENTS

INTRODUCTION

The journey to health is not all about food. It's not easy, it varies for everyone and it's always imperfect. You can't get a one-way ticket and travel down a singular path to reach an end. Healing is not linear. It is a constant exploration of mind, body and soul.

This book is about merging the conversation between food and wellness. Awakening the senses through beautiful and delicious recipes that are not only here to nourish you but to heal you. Mello is here to electrify your relationship with your inner self as well as your relationship with food, and develop a deeper connection to holistic healing.

Food can be a form of healing, but it is just one part of a whole. The writings within this book connect the healing powers of food with overall wellness, creating a guide to help you live your best and most radiant life. Food can be a meditative release and a pleasure, but food is often abused and or neglected in our society. Each page of this book will have information to help you learn to embrace a healthy relationship with food and yourself.

Mello is here to give you independence, confidence, better relationships, deeper connections and a stronger appreciation for your whole self. Cooking can be a useful tool when it comes to healing and I have found myself in a deep meditative state from being in the kitchen and by changing the foods that I choose to nurture my body with. You literally are what you eat, and if you fuel your body with vibrant, living, whole plant based foods you will shine from within.

You can feel better and I want to show you how. What you choose to put in your body can not only impact your physical body but has a profound effect on your mind as well. I have experienced so many facets of myself over the years. Coming to a place where my relationship with food is balanced, has been life long. There have been points where I ate whatever I wanted, and then ran and ran and ran until shin splints stopped me. My mind assuming that since I worked out so much I could eat endless calories. I have struggled deeply with restriction, binging and a number of other self deprecating habits, all that pointed back to an unhealthy relationship with food. Along the way I would lose weight, then gain it back, but whether I lost or gained I felt the same. This brought me to a point where I was deeply enthralled by food and perplexed by its effects on me. It took years for me to stop visualizing diet as just that, a diet. I spent extensive time dancing between obsession and fear all revolving around the food on my plate.

The obvious answer was right in front of me all along. It all matters, all changes begin from within, and anything you want to manifest needs to come from a genuine place. You absolutely cannot listen to anyone, you must trust your own intuition. My hope is that Mello can guide you back to the core of your own being.

Through trial and error, a lot of reading, conversation and education, I found that eating in harmony with your personal needs could very well alter you as a person. Removing restrictive tendencies, toxic relationships with food, eliminating processed foods, hormones, GMO's, refined sugars, chemicals, dairy and inflammatory foods can quite literally change you. By adapting a whole foods plant based diet you can quickly connect deeply to a part of yourself that you might not even know exists. It may seem ridiculous when you hear someone say that eating kale changed their life. Yet there is truth in this. Food does have the capability to create incredible shifts in your overall health. This book is meant to be a tool for you to utilize on your journey towards vibrant health and wellness.

"Veganism is not about giving anything up or losing anything; it is about gaining the peace within yourself that comes from embracing nonviolence and refusing to participate in the exploitation of the vulnerable" Gary L. Francione

Food can be a joyful experience, whether you are cooking or eating, it encompasses incredible forms of healing for your whole being. Feeding people is one of the greatest acts of love. As I began properly caring for my body I started to feel an undeniable yearning to share with others. Gathering and sharing around a table filled with foods that cultivate brilliant health is a wonderful step towards healing.

Mello was a state of mind that came to life as I spent more time in the kitchen, in harmony with real foods that were giving me life. I have had so many peaceful moments in the kitchen, cooking and preparing, sharing abundance and life through healing foods.

You can take back your health and your well-being. Mello is here to make you feel empowered through your life, your journey and your choices. By encouraging you to love yourself through and through by sharing and cultivating your experiences with food, spiritual and mental healing and opportunities that arise. Guiding you in living your own life, your best life and aiding in making the connection between your diet, lifestyle and mental well-being.

THE JOURNEY

Are you tired of feeling sick? Do you feel a calling within you to make a difference in the world? Whatever it is that you are feeling, if you are reading these pages you are ready for a new beginning. Something inside of you has shifted and you are officially open to change. The words and recipes within this book are here to nourish and inspire along the way. However, it is up to you to implement my suggestions and manifest your reality. You deserve this, we can work together to get you there.

The passage to health is mental, physical and spiritual. Thriving successfully in a life of abundance, longevity, and well-being comes from working on yourself internally as well as externally. Your journey is more than the stunning foods found among these pages. It is an everyday discovery of self love and cultivated joy. In sharing my personal story and wisdom that has been passed down along the way my hope is that you find inspiration for your own voyage into healing.

This is a plant based cookbook filled with loving words and soulful recipes. However this book found you, I hope that it serves you. I hope that this fills you up and encourages you to be all that you intrinsically are.

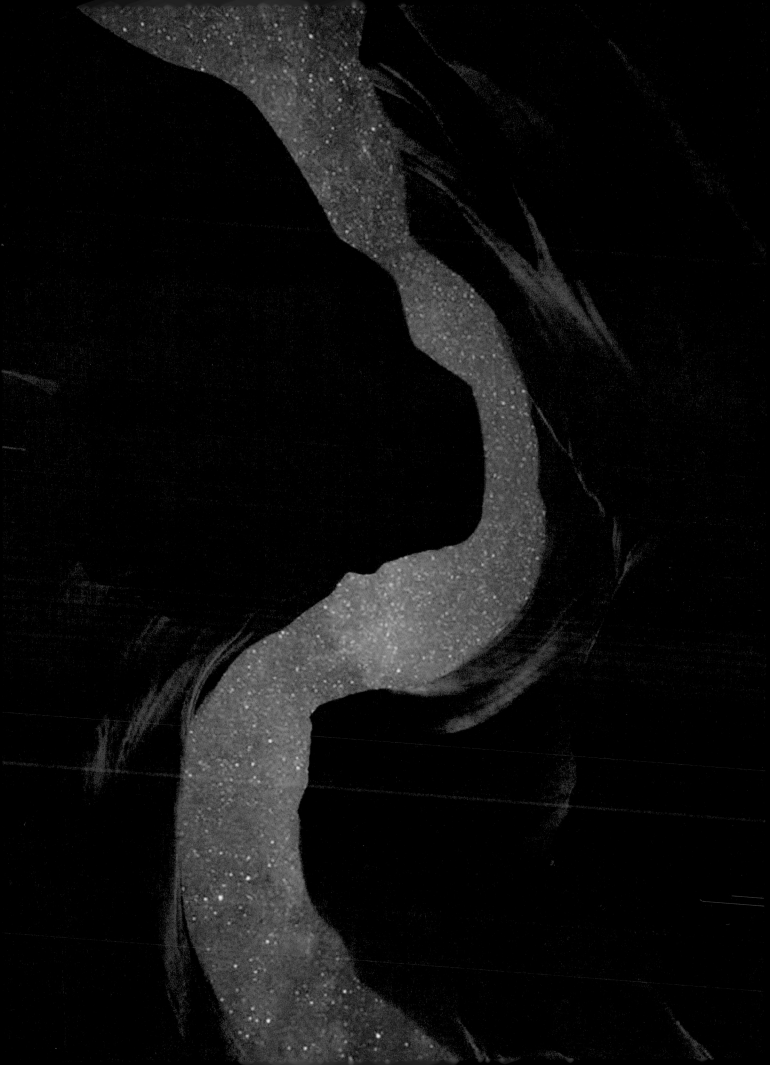

PHYSICAL

PHYSICAL

It has taken a lot for me to sit down and write about my journey to
self confidence. There were so many moments where I sat down,
with intentions to let it all out, and ended up staring at a blank screen
unsure how to arrange all of my emotions into coherent thoughts.
So often all of those who follow me on Social Media see the bright
colorful food, the big smiles, the golden light. It can all be deceiving
and obscure the present reality of someones life.

There was a point in my life where a simple task, like getting dressed
in the morning, could make or break my day. I remember standing
there disgusted with my reflection. I would constantly reach for darker
colors and looser fitting pieces. It took me until I was 26 years old to
realize that the mirror was not my enemy, I was. This is the case for
so many of us. Female and male. It is programed into us to ridicule
ourselves until we break and it takes time, work and courage to get
rid of that programming and replace it with thoughts of love and
appreciation for the incredible body in front of us.

Imagine standing in the mirror and not thinking twice about it. Not
questioning the reflection, and dismissing the urge to reach for a
different outfit. Why don't we just smile at ourselves, embrace our
differences and feel the beauty that radiates out of us? This should
be what we do every single day instead of telling ourselves we aren't
good enough, skinny enough, fit enough, tall enough etc. You don't
have to be anything other than what you are.

You just need to be, beautiful you.

Try just taking a picture. Set a timer and just take a picture of you. No
filters, no angels, no poses. I did this and at first I felt—uncomfortable
and so awkward. The insecurity overwhelmed me. I picked myself
apart. But then something unexpected happened. I felt bad for myself.
But not because the way I looked, I felt bad because when I looked
harder at the person and the photo in front of me I began to see past
that voice. I felt guilty, responsible for all the bad thoughts I ever had,
the pressure I put on myself and the pain I put myself through. It hurt
me to finally see someone, so beautiful and so special, a version of
me that I truly never took the time to see because I was so utterly
consumed by all the darkness and self loathing. I saw ME. A beautiful
girl with a beautiful heart who wants nothing more then to be happy
and feel at home in her own skin. In this moment I looked at myself
and I felt peace, I felt like I came home.

We all compare ourselves to others, and I am guilty of that myself. We are not just bodies, we are beings. Beings with souls, hearts, emotions, needs and flaws...just like every creature on Earth.

Today when I look in the mirror I smile at myself and I feel beautiful.

How did I get to this moment? What universe am I living in and how do I take you there? Honestly it is simple, I stopped caring. I spent years being painfully addicted to food as well as exercise. I always struggled with over indulging, binging, stuffing my face like the world was going to end all because I was so concerned about how I was going to be perceived. I let it go. I embraced myself as I am right now. I embraced health and by doing so began to see my body as a friend, not an enemy.

You are beautiful and you are capable of seeing and celebrating that beauty. Spend time speaking loving words to yourself rather than hateful. See your flaws, scars, wounds and hold them closer to you. Begin slowly. So much of our perception is dictated by the voices we heard growing up. Trauma we don't even know we carry. It is a marathon not a sprint on this path to healing our confidence.

Begin. No matter how small. Begin. You deserve to see your own innate beauty.

HEALING HISTORY

I grew up in a household where everyday revolved around food. There would be yelling if a plate was not completely cleaned of every morsel of food. I spent my youth in the kitchen with my Nana and my mother. Nana grew up on a farm in Italy, she had a deep love for food but much of it was from a dated mentality, filled with unhealthy patterns that were passed down to me.

She lived with us for 10 years and during that time I learned how to cook, set tables and clean up. I was automatically put in what many would consider a typical "female role". My brother was able to go and play with his friends, get outside and practice sports and in essence be a well rounded healthy child.

I was in the kitchen with Nana day in and day out and I began associating food with everything. I never thought of how much I was consuming. I would often eat to the point that I felt ill. My Nana unknowingly created a lot of this binging behavior by scolding me to eat more, needing me to be her taste tester and creating fear around not finishing a plate of food. Then shame from the fact that if my Brother did not clear his own plate I would be told to finish it for him. All of this shaped my relationship with eating and food. Making me both fear it and depend on it all at the same time.

As time passed I noticed I was gaining weight. I did not look like other people in my family. I was heavier and felt deeply fatigued which made me incredibly insecure. My relatives could eat whatever they wanted and look petite and feminine, while I battled with the reflection in the mirror staring back at me. At one point I wondered if I was meant to be a boy.

My relationship with food became even more mangled as time went on. As we got older my brother started wanting processed foods that were not a norm in our household. This kind of food soon became a staple in the home for him and his friends. I was told time and time again that I was not allowed to eat these foods. This put me in a spiral of shame. Shame that lead me to seek revenge by harming my own body.

There were days I would take the frozen junk food and eat it alone in the bathroom, often partially frozen just because I knew I was barred from having it.

I knew it was a bad choice for my own being but it was my way of trying to gain control over a body I felt disconnected from.

The embarrassment and hatred I felt for myself started to extend into other areas of my life. I started becoming very aware of my weight and I didn't like it. I used to stand in the mirror and grab the excess skin and fat on my body.

I would squeeze it as hard as I could out of anger and frustration, wishing I could just rip it off. Then I would come down stairs, eat more food and my grandma would hold up her pinky and say, "you have to be skinny like this for the boys" or "why aren't you thin like your cousins" or "you look fat."

My way of fighting through the self loathing was to turn to sports. When I was younger I had practiced dance, specifically ballet and I loved it. One day that changed when a girl grabbed my armpit fat and said, "why do you have this?" I never went back. By the time I was in high school I had tried a whole range of sports, except basketball. I did them because I saw no other outlet for my body. I figured if I ran far enough, jumped high enough that my body would somehow become one that I deemed worthy of love.

These vicious cycles of eating out of boredom, stress, anxiety, yelling, or pleasure continued until I was about 21 years old. Then something clicked within me and I started to ask questions.

I met yet another roadblock as I began to develop more and more queries. Western Medicine has its place. But when it comes to nutrition and general wellness they lack education and our system is set up for it to be financially beneficial for you to stay unwell. Doctors I would seek help from would tell me I was overweight but would give me no concrete help in how to alter that. My therapist was urging me to be put on medication and my gynecologist thought the only way to balance my hormones was to start birth control.

I struggled at first to assert my voice. To question them. To do my own research. All I knew for sure was I did not want to feel like I was feeling any longer. It was a long road. But overtime I learned not to take myself for granted. I began to love even the darkest spaces of my soul. I found my voice.

I wish this for all of you. To come to a point of healing. A point of knowing your own value and worth. We all experience trauma that was never intended to hurt us. We all must heal from the voices of ours pasts. We must learn to forge forward with determination to find a healthier space of living for our own bodies and hearts. You are priceless. And you deserve to love yourself fully. Let's begin together.

BEGINNING

Before I opened up my mind and my heart I used to associate happy people with complete sociopaths. If you were a person sharing health, positive vibes, an active lifestyle, or veganism I dismissed you entirely and probably made fun of you. I told myself over and over again that I was fine. Content. And would never fall into the wellness world in a million years.

Yet here I am, years later, writing these words, hoping to instill something in you that encourages you in a way that I always needed and never really had.

It's funny, sometimes the things that we question are beneficial to us. All those years I resented people for changing, growing and evolving. I pushed them away because I did not feel worthy of their relationship and I created toxic self deprecating situations, all containing outcomes that would just dig a deeper hole for me and my self loathing.

I was in a toxic relationship with myself, headed down a road leading nowhere and everything in me had completely and totally given up-- yet deep down all I ever wanted was to be happy, to feel appreciated and to be loved. If I could fix one small thing in my life it would be finding happiness--but happiness is not just one small thing, it is everything.

We all have a common feeling, we want to live happy and healthy lives and we yearn to feel appreciated and loved. These days, health is the new wealth and happiness is the new rich. Everywhere you look you can find someone advocating for self love and self care, preaching the benefits of loving themselves and sharing their grand reawakening while sitting in a candle lit bath.

We all know that self care and love are essential to a healthy lifestyle. But we are being fed by industries telling us exactly what that should look like. We get caught up in indulgent beauty products, expensive exercise clothing and other materialistic goods that will apparently bring us unadulterated joy.

At the end of the day you and I both know that you cannot pay for happiness. It is not a place you can go visit, you can not earn it, or consume it. Happiness is internal and comes from your soul.

My own story of finding my way to the kitchen started a while back before I knew myself, my dreams and most importantly the calling of my own heart. Before I found the calling to create I was sitting in class on my way to becoming a Radiologic Technician. I realized during my first week that something was very off. Everyone around me was excited. Bursting at the seams with plans for the future and interest in the subject. And I felt numb. Bored. Completely unhappy with where I was going.

Every night I tried to fall into it. Organizing my notes and folders, color coding my class sheets. Moment by moment attempting to convince myself that this is where I wanted to be. I told myself that in 2 years I would be totally done with school, I would be free. I would have a good, reliable job and I would be living a great life. No matter how much I talked myself into it, I knew at the core of me this was not the path for me.

All this time I had been pushing myself down a road that was not meant for me. I was focusing too much on pleasing others, making my family happy and having what I knew would be considered a steady job.

Instead of realizing the beauty of my own talents, I fought against them. The universe kept guiding me towards creative and manual careers and yet I still tried to become something I was not.

One night the voice inside my head had finally driven me to the breaking point. I knew I needed an outside source to help me reach the conclusion I already knew within. I asked my boyfriend Derek what he thought I should do. I knew he would tell me to leave the course and pursue a creative endeavor, but I really just needed to hear it from him in order to go through with it.

That night I withdrew from the Radiography program at County College of Morris and I contacted an art school. I applied to one school, Otis College of Art and Design, and in a matter of 48 hours I talked to my parents about how I actually felt. I made a portfolio with the help of Derek and I applied.

I felt like I could breathe again, but I also felt a rush of negative emotions.

I felt like a failure, I felt anxious, sad, embarrassed--but none of that mattered because I was happier and it was all because I stepped out of my comfort zone. I focused on my breath, my voice and my needs and I realized that ultimately this was my life. No one else's.

A massive shift occurred and I began to make much bigger shifts in my subconscious mind. One by one I dismissed my self limiting beliefs, traded in my negative mindset and opted for a brighter one. Changed my lifestyle--transitioning to a plant based diet, and challenged my fears. I reached a point where I was really frustrated with not feeling like I was enough and I knew these shifts were essential for my own evolution.

We ebb and flow through many transitions. So consumed with seeking answers and attaining moments of happiness that we often miss out on what are actual wants and needs are. We neglect aspects of our lives, to make room for unrealistic goals, fake dreams and materialistic possessions. We spend too much money and waste too much time, attaching our psyche to filtered images online and daydreaming about artificial bodies filled with manipulated happiness. We dream, desire and want instead of listening, learning and understanding our needs.

External validation is a poison. When we look to other people and compare ourselves all while attempting to emulate them, we lose contact with our true selves. Searching for validation from others by looking for attention, trying to live up to other people's standards and/or giving into societal pressure is a very real and dark trouble that many men and women deal with on a day to day basis.

We need to actively unlearn unhealthy patterns ingrained in us from a young age. This regards practices ranging from proper diet, to body image, to supplementation and mental health.

I want to encourage you to rise. Rise from programmed to elevated, and be all that you wish to be. But do so in a way that does not compromise your well-being because all aspects of health matter and that includes mental, physical and spiritual.

The trinity of elements that encompass a healthy life were what I focused on in order to forge a path to becoming the person I am today.

True health and happiness is not just about the food you eat, the job you have or the clothes you wear. It is about balancing all aspects of your whole self. Mental, Spiritual and physical health. Finding a way to nourish them all in a way that works for you and your lifestyle. Walk away from all that does not serve and fuel your heart with passion. There are so many paths. So many choices. Believe in your own abilities and talents. Do this and I promise you will experience incredible moments within a truly happy and healthy life.

MENTALITY

Our minds are a powerful force, the conscious and subconscious mind sanctioning our ability to function as human beings. Be aware and appreciative for all of your abilities—Don't ever let your 'weaknesses' hold you back from living. Your weaknesses are just an obstacle of your subconscious mind--preventing you from harnessing your full potential. The thoughts and doubts that hold us back from doing certain things or responding a certain way.

If you are not happy and you are finding that you are craving change, peace, well-being, strength and understanding...you are in the right place. You have all that you need within you, inside of your beautiful and chaotic mind, to realign your life in a way that truly serves you. It is up to you, and only you to create active change in your life.

Your thoughts can directly influence how you feel overall. In order to create a shift in your daily life start by changing the way you speak to yourself. Instead of feeding into your fears, feed into your courage. Push yourself past your comfort zone, stop holding yourself back, let go of anything that does not light you up from the inside out. We often think that searching for more will lead us to abundance, but in reality, being grateful and appreciating our lives and its transitions is they key to feeling more at peace. Mental health is the building block for spiritual and physical health. One of the crucial elements that leads us to better well-being is understanding how important it is to have a relationship with ourselves.

In order to feel mentally strong, physically able and spiritually connected, you will need to put in work in all aspects of your life, not just parts of it.

We have been created to be powerful and ever-changing forces, each of us traveling down unique and personalized paths. Like butterflies, we are transformative--constantly changing and evolving—growing and vibrating at different frequencies.

We are exceptional, but we repeatedly forget our superpowers. We fail to use our eyes to actually see that we are each truly irreplaceable and we lose sight of how far we've come. This is my ultimate weakness.

Your presence is your superpower. Your beating heart is your rhythm and your breath is your peace. Hear the voice in your mind, but do not listen.

We are very hard on ourselves because we can be--we tear ourselves down, struggling internally, revolving around our own little universes feeling like we are not enough. But you are enough...you are more. We all matter. All shapes, all beings, all souls. We all have feelings, needs, dreams, fears, desires, weaknesses.

I believe that in order to reach fitness goals, life goals, career goals, personal goals you need to have a proper relationship with yourself. This means you need to have a genuine understanding of who you are working with.

I have always done my best to remain self aware. I have a big heart and a soul that longs to always love more and discover new facets of itself. Unfortunately the reality of having a big heart is often putting others before yourself which can lead to burnout and exhaustion.

We all have hearts, some bigger than others—but the people with the biggest hearts tend to spread themselves the thinnest. We shift our perspectives with the intent to understand more so than to respond, we forget to say no and fail to speak our truth in fear of hurting someone else's emotions. We pour ourselves into everything we do. Loving hard...but forgetting that not every creature shares this beautiful gift of ours.

We have often been told we are too emotional, care too much or take things to heart--but that is our superpower. We are wise and we are like water. Bodies of water are expansive in their depth. The surface only revealing a fragment of what lies beneath.

From dreams to intuition, magic and mystery, water holds endless inspiration. Our sensitive souls are unique in the way in which they love and feel. What we may consider weakness is actually incredible strength.

If you are a sensitive person utilize your sensitivity to build the life of your dreams. Build your world around you to be whatever you want it to be. By embracing the love and compassion and leaving fear behind you will achieve all that it is you put your mind too.

Negative emotions, anxiety, self doubt these are all cynical instincts that constrain us from moving forward—and we all feel this on some level. Developing conscious knowledge of the emotions that visit you regularly is essential in evolving one's mental health.

Whether you realize it or not, you are responsible for bringing both positive and negative influences into your life. By placing your focus on negative emotions and feelings, (living in the past, guilt, distrust, jealousy, judgment, negative 'pressures') you hold yourself back, strain your external bonds and bring your dreams to a halt.

You have the power to control your response and regulate your emotions. If you look for the silver lining in every moment then you'll soon start to see the goodness and the beauty surrounding every good day and bad day. Being aware of your thoughts and how their impact your well being can solidify the knowledge that you have the ability to free yourself and take control of your mind. You can obtain what you desire.

The mind is a complex beast. Some days you will be able to find your breath. You will be able to calm your racing mind and find your moments of peace and clarity. Other days will be harder. The anxiety can come back when triggered at full force. Be gentle with yourself. This is not about perfection rather about healing. Slowly. Thoughtfully. And truly healing. I personally aim to take one day at a time. I focus on the present moment and I let go of what I cannot control. Listen to the cues of your mind, body and spirit. You will get there.

One of the most incredible tools for a balanced mind is finding your breath. Your breath is your life force, an element of your life that you can master.

Controlling your breath awakens your subconscious mind and generates an oasis of stillness. This moment of center can aid in managing an anxiety attack. The majority of what is holding you back spawns from internal forces generated from the mind. Only you can control your own actions and reactions, no one else. Please know that anxiety is a mental health condition and these practices are for self care. Please seek the help of a professional to truly conquer mental health battles.

If your heart is racing and you are feeling anxious, close your eyes and focus on your breath. Breathe in through your nose, make this breath long, deep and slow. Exhale out of your nose with a conscious effort to extend the breath leaving your body, imagine waves, or water—the sound will be just like that. The constriction in your throat creates a calming, whispering breath, soft, deep, warm. You will feel a sense of comfort and control. Repeat for as short as a minute, to as long as an hour. Be still and be patient.

This whispering breath, will serve in eliminating negative emotions, worry, anxiousness, as well as helping you reach a calmer state of mind. Let it all go. You are in control and all of these negative inclinations are just a compulsion blurring the lines between a dark and scattered mind and true presence.

I used fear that I was mentally and emotionally incapable of anything that truly mattered. I kept to myself, my ego apprehensive to any form of spotlight. My opinions remained silent and I continuously feared loss. I was so afraid. Afraid that at any given moment I'd be 'figured out' and people would see that I was boring, too silent. I was afraid of not being enough.

I found myself in isolation, closing off my heart to anything that questioned my current lifestyle.

I was terrified of my own inner light. I have come a long way and I have certainly evolved into a person who no longer fears the way people view me.. I no longer fear my emotions, myself or my purpose.

As I steadily move past the mark of a year, from the time I made the commitment to focus full time on me and my love to help others the thoughts in my mind sometimes creep back.

My mind challenges me and pushes me each day, questioning everything, analyzing all of it and attempting to tear down these strong walls of confidence and resilience that I have built—but I am stronger. My love for giving, nourishing and encouraging others and myself runs deeper than any negative thought I have ever had.

I no longer fear what people think and despite what my mind second guesses during moments of weakness—I know this. I no longer yearn for a life where people like me, or leave me alone entirely—I am me.

There are still times when my insecurities are really put on the line, there is always going to be something that triggers you. My anxiety resurfaces and I feel just as terrified of my own thoughts as I once did. Surrounded by my deepest fears, I freeze, panic and cringe. I recoil at the fact that for a glimpse of a moment I thought I was better. But then moments of clarity as I relish in the knowledge that healing is not linear. It does not stop and start. It is continuous. Ever changing. Ever in transition. There will be good days and bad days. Days where I feel like I can take on the world and days where I need to ask for extra support. All of it is part of the process of healing.

Go where you want to go, explore your interests and all of life's possibilities. Life is a beautiful thing and many people let it slip away. The most rewarding feeling is knowing you took a risk and stepped out of your comfort zone. Challenging yourself is not only going to make you stronger but it will build up your confidence.

Take a step towards evolving and growing by embracing your superpowers, feeling your emotions, understanding them and doing whatever you need to do in order to be truly happy on a daily basis. Remove toxicity, inhale all the goodness around you and count your blessings.

Exhale the rest and let that shit go.

There is no limit to what you can do and no matter what shape you want your life to take, I want you to know that you can have all the things you see in your mind. Feed your imagination and cast your dreams and desires into the universe with daily.

Your imagination is infinite, and so are your abilities.

SPIRITUAL

"When we identify with the small ego-centered self this is called relative reality, because that small self is prone to change. When we realize that there is a subtler, permanent reality behind the relative one and we see that our true nature is pure unlimited consciousness, this is known as Self Realization."

-Dada Nabhaniilananda

Be present. For this is the only place where life exists. There is a difference between happiness and being present. Almost everybody wants to be happy, and that means different things for different people. However, our perception of what happiness is, can be very jaded. The reason for this is because we are constantly looking towards the next moment, waiting for the "when" the "if" that magical (non existent) moment where everything will just click. There is no such thing as perfect timing. But why do we need to reach that threshold? Why not just experience the sensation of happiness right now?

A critical element of finding yourself in the moment is cultivating activities that enhance your spiritual, mental and physical development. My yoga practice has deeply connected me to my presence, generating so much growth in daily life. My practice has evolved my entire being, reconnected me to my inner peace and introduced my heart to a new form of gathering.

Yoga began as a way for me to disconnect and find solitude. I was able to be at one with my body and find peace within my mind. I did not engage with those around me and my introverted personality remained especially closed off when I entered a room. When I began to understand that yoga begins when you walk out the door, I started to feel truly alive for the first time. There is life before a class, where I would feel anxious, scattered and scared and then there was life after a class when I felt unbreakable--fearless and strong.

Sharing space and connecting energy with a community of souls that are all meant to be in a specific place at a specific time is absolutely magical. The chance and opportunity that we all end up in the same room, practicing at the same time--despite our days and responsibilities--is such a gift.

This community, has granted me the ability to navigate through my emotions and integrate my feelings in a way where I can feel my body, as it is, and truly be in the now. My breath as I flow from pose to pose has showed me how I can work through pain and discomfort, simply by harnessing this life force and channeling the whispering breath in a way that ignites a fire within me.

There is no judgment here, there is no perfect moment, pose or climactic moment. There is just imperfectly perfect transition, in a room full of bodies--souls--all linked through different rhythms. Breath rolling in and out just as waves come in with the tide. We are one. I feel held here, whole, synced to my inherent nature. My healing has never been linear, as it shouldn't be and my constant exploration of mind, body and soul has taken me down so many winding roads.

Instead of following, existing and accepting I started listening, understanding and trying. This lead me back home to my body. My yoga practice truly gives me butterflies, makes me feel unstoppable and is actively aiding in weight loss, maintaining strength and leading a healthy life.

What makes you happy and truly lights a fire within you? For me that was letting go of the pressure I had on myself, finding a way to move my body that was more instinctual and less force of habit.

I let my body guide me, and for a while I did not follow any kind of routine I just made sure to move for 30 minutes a day, each day and I kept listening intently. After some time I now know what my body needs and craves and can rise to fulfill those needs daily. I have learned the importance of knowing when to work out my physical body. As well as when to work in, diving inward and working on my inner peace.

I have found something to feed my soul and I am feeling elated by the way the universe has brought this practice into my life. For the longest time everything around me grew, transformed and revolved around food. Just as I filled moments of joy with beautiful meals, I also filled an emptiness with overindulgent binges and spiraling obsession. My previous ways of combating the self loathing never solved anything. Through yoga I have been able to realign my thoughts, energy and focus and while discovering a new facet of myself.

The unison of body, mind and spirit that is essential within a practice is everything that ignited my passion to add these words to this book. Yoga quite literally means to join, or unite together. By aligning so many elements in my life I was able to reconnect to my relationship with food in a positive way, a more sustainable way.

I am grateful, I am embracing and feeling my body, I am implementing positive actions and habits into my life and for the first time my soul craves connection. Gathering around a table and sharing a meal together is rooted within my being, except now I feed and nourish my body, I feed my imagination and appreciate my mind, and I feed my spiritual universe. All of these things are growing to encompass the trinity of elements that grants me the ability to lead a healthy and fulfilling life.

By connecting with my spirituality I have deepened my mindfulness and compassion for myself, the world around me and for others.

I no longer live in a trance of harmful thought, unable to visualize my truth. Reaching inner resolve was something that awakened in my practice. As I worked through my transitions and struggled with holding poses I was met face to face with emotions and self deprecating thoughts that had been buried in my mind for years.

All of my feelings of deficiency were right there with me on my mat as if they were an invisible gas filling up my lungs, suffocating me.

For a while I felt imprisoned in my thoughts, what began as a way for me to disconnect and find solitude, was suddenly a cage. I no longer felt at peace on my mat and that was when I truly felt all of the inner rejection I had for myself. My mental health and spiritual enlightenment had merged and I was being challenged by everything all at once.

By building a stronger relationship with my mind I was able to endure. Through harnessing my breath and I was driven to feel the light. I faced all the painful thoughts. Addiction to food, my fear of people, fear of connection and acceptance.

Some weeks I would go everyday, sometimes twice a day. There would be classes where I would just lay there and cry. At first I felt embarrassed, but with the heat of the class it just looked like I was sweating. As I got closer to myself I did not care, I started to feed my mind with self love, sweet words and calming thoughts. I practiced my breathing, I listened to the deep sound within the base of my throat and I focused.

There were many classes where it was so difficult to sort through the thoughts that I would shut them off. I would focus on my breath and just be. My presence on my mat became my strength and my superpower and by showing up to a class, despite my emotional state, I was taking care of me. I re-grounded myself through my practice. I learned how to really digest my thoughts, understand them, breath with them, or shut them off entirely. There is a reflection of infinite within our minds, a mirror to limitless consciousness that is constant and eternal. This reflection can be uncovered at the core of our true spiritual self. I had experienced the different levels of my inner being, disconnecting from what we identify as, our ego, by directly connecting to my mental and physical nature.

Self realization ignited my yoga practice and granted me mental and physical peace. Uniting me with my higher self. I continue practicing this in my daily life through being grateful, moving my body in a way that serves me (my yoga practice) and sharing love and abundance.

This book is a result of discovering new parts of myself. Connecting my love of food as nourishment, movement and spirituality. Each word a small piece of me that I am honored to share with you.

I want to share with you some small daily integrations that can help you form a relationship with a spiritual side of yourself. Connecting you and grounding you to all that exists in this world.

Be grateful Wake up, and actively search your mind for everything that you are grateful for. You will be surprised at just how much fills your life. Focus on the things we so often forget. Running water, shelter, hands that allow us to type, a mind that allows us to read. A kiss from your partner. A hug from a friend. A flower growing up through concrete. Focus on these small gifts and you will begin to realize how much light surrounds you.

Exercise Move your body, every morning. When I wake up I like to do some kind of movement to ease my body into the day. One of my favorite ways to energize my soul is by taking a hot yoga class. How you choose to move is entirely up to you. Just allowing yourself to move, even for 10 minutes can make all the difference. These moments feeling your body move will become a habit that will set your mood for the day ahead.

Be kind Implement positive habits and actions into your life. Kindness can be given everyday. Focusing less on yourself and more of your attention towards little acts of kindness will actually give you more peace within yourself and connect you with so many brilliant souls.

My whole life I lived in pain. I lived in sadness, doubt and loneliness. I settled and accepted, cried and played victim. I let life consume me and swallow me whole without taking a chance to breathe for myself and forge a path articulated with care and heart for myself.

I dismissed my options, I pushed away people and I closed off my heart to the world. I gave up and I gave in.

Now I live in constant passion. Passion for myself, for others and for life and love. Everything I have given you is a piece of myself and the ways in which I have healed myself.

I started my journey for me and now I am here to encourage you on your own journey to growth and self discovery. You can pick and choose what resonates with you. Create the recipes that fuel your body best, find a practice that enlivens your body and soul. It is all up to you and I so look forward to hearing about your own adventure with yourself.

"The prerequisite to true freedom is to decide that you do not want to suffer anymore. You must decide that you want to enjoy your life and that there is no reason for stress, inner pain, or fear.

Every day we bear a burden that we should not be bearing. We fear that we are not good enough, strong enough or that we will fail. We experience insecurity, anxiety, and self consciousness. We fear that people will turn on us, take advantage of us or stop loving us.

As we try to succeed and express ourselves, there is an inner weight that we carry. This weight is the fear of experiencing pain, anguish, or sorrow. Every day we are either feeling it, or we are protecting ourselves from feeling it. It is such a core influence that we don't even realize how prevalent it is."

Michael A. Singer The Untethered Soul

This book is here to support you, to guide you and to nurture you. My intentions have always been about helping people in the least intimidating way. We are human and our bodies are a blessing. It's okay to take time to nurture yourself in whatever way feels best.

That may be expressing yourself externally to others, finding solitude, or diving inward. It could also be anything in between. Trust yourself. Only you know what is best for you in order to heal. You don't need to follow any protocol or fit the expectations of others. Follow your gut, your heart, and your inner voice.

Whatever phase you are at in your journey, whether it be self love, mental health, spiritual growth, fitness or all the above, remember you are such a gift and you are lucky to have you.

Enjoy your process and introduce lifestyle changes that truly motivate you and excite you. Your transitions are just as important as your checkpoints. Your well being is more important than a number on a scale, pleasing anyone but yourself or sacrificing your happiness. In order to live a healthy, happy life it all matters.

You have all of the answers that you could possibly need within you. Embrace this, love the body you inhabit, flaws, cellulite, stretch marks, hair and all because who cares? No one. Except that judgmental voice in your head and you have the power to hear it, change it and make a shift. Don't let that inner voice over power your dreams.

Here is to new beginnings. Loving ourselves fully. Fueling our magnificent human minds with never ending growth. You are capable of all things and I hope this book serves as a continuous reminder of that. I cannot wait to see what you give to this world. What you give to yourself. To a future full of gathering. Nourishment. Laughter. And overall an all encompassing love.

Food can be a form of healing, but it is just a small part of it. You can take back your health and your well-being,You can feel better and I hope that Mello can inspire you along the way. Thank you for exploring this world with me. Enjoy every page and I hope you find ones you go back too time and time again.

I love you, even if I do not know you because I know you are a soul that deserves to shine and I support you endlessly. My heart is with you, always and I will never give up on you, even when you give up on yourself.

Love your fellow hungry bunny,
Gianna

ESSENTIAL

NACHO CHEESE

Prep Time: 5 min | Total Time: 10 min | Serves: 10-13 Hungry Bunnies

NGREDIENTS

. C cashews, soaked overnight
4 oz roasted green Chiles
½-1 C water
2-3 Tbs nutritional Yeast
½ jalapeño, optional
¼ C mild salsa
.-2 Tbs apple Cider Vinegar
. clove garlic

INSTRUCTIONS

1. Add all ingredients into your Vitamix or high-speed blender and blend until thick and creamy.

2. Add more liquid if necessary. If you would like a thinner sauce then start off with ½ C of water. If you are not using a vitamix you will need the full cup.

BBQ SAUCE

Prep Time: 10 min | Total Time: 30 min | Serves: 10-13 Hungry Bunnies

NGREDIENTS

: Tbs low sodium vegetable broth
-5 cloves of garlic chopped
 onion chopped
 C ketchup
/3 C molasses
/3 C coconut sugar
/4 C low sodium veggie broth
. Tbs apple cider vinegar
. Tbs Worcestershire sauce
. Tbs liquid smoke
/4 tsp black pepper

NSTRUCTIONS

1. Sauté onions and garlic in the olive oil until golden brown and slightly over done.

2. Add ketchup, molasses, coconut sugar, veggie broth, apple cider vinegar, Worcestershire sauce, liquid smoke.

3. Simmer for 15-20 minutes, then transfer to a high speed blender and blend until smooth.

CASHEW CREAM

Prep Time: 5 min | Total Time: 5 min | Serves: 10-13 Hungry Bunnies

INGREDIENTS

2 C cashews
2 C water

INSTRUCTIONS

1. Add all ingredients into your Vitamix or high-speed blender and blend until thick and creamy.

CASHEW MAYO

Prep Time: 5 min | Total Time: 10 min | Serves: 10-13 Hungry Bunnies

INGREDIENTS

1 C cashews, soaked overnight
½ C water
1 large lemon, peeled, sliced, and seeded
¼ tsp pink Himalayan salt
2 Tbs apple cider vinegar
½ tsp ground mustard
¼ C chickpeas, rinsed and drained
1 clove garlic, chopped (optional)

INSTRUCTIONS

1. Add all ingredients into your Vitamix or high-speed blender and blend until thick and creamy.

ORANGE CHIPOTLE MAYO

Prep Time: 5 min | Total Time: 10 min | Serves: 10-13 Hungry Bunnies

INGREDIENTS

1 C cashew mayo
3 Tbs orange juice + the zest
1 Tbs chipotle Chiles, canned

INSTRUCTIONS

1. Add all ingredients into your Vitamix or high-speed blender and blend until thick and creamy.

2. Add more liquid if necessary. If you would like a thinner sauce then start off with ½ C of water. If you are not using a vitamix you will need the full cup.

RAW SLAW

Prep Time: 10 min | Total Time: 10 min | Serves: 6-8 Hungry Bunnies

INGREDIENTS

4 C shredded purple cabbage
1 C shredded carrots
1 C shredded apple
1 L beet
1-2 oranges, juiced + zest
¼ C apple cider vinegar
2 Tbs maple syrup
¼ tsp dry mustard
¼ tsp ground celery seed
¼ tsp sea salt
¼ tsp black pepper

INSTRUCTIONS

1. In a large bowl toss together shredded cabbage, apple, beet and carrots.

2. Combine all the other ingredients in a small bowl. Pour dressing over cabbage mixture and toss to coat. Let mixture sit for at least 10 minutes in the fridge, stir and serve.

VEGETABLE BROTH

Prep Time: 10 min | Total Time: 1 hour | Serves: 10 Hungry Bunnies

INGREDIENTS

1 Tbsp water
1 onion with the skin, shredded
1 head/bulb of celery chopped small
4 medium carrots chopped small
9-10 C water
1 C chopped kale
1 garlic bulb smashed
½ cup chopped fresh parsley
1 fresh thyme, basil, parsley, rosemary,
handful of each of these
2 whole bay leaves
½ lb turnips, cubed
4-5 Tbsp pureed roasted tomatoes
2 tbsp ground turmeric
*optional, but adds a lot of flavor
S+P to taste

INSTRUCTIONS

1. In a large pot over medium heat. Add water, onion, garlic, carrots, and celery. Sauté for about 5 minutes or until softened and slightly browned, stirring frequently.

2. Add water, along with everything else and increase heat to medium high until the mixture comes to a boil. Then reduce to a simmer and stir to combine and loosely cover, cook for 1 hour.

3. Taste and adjust seasoning before serving or utilizing.

ROASTED TOMATOES

Prep Time: 20 min | Total Time: 1 hour | Serves: 10 Hungry Bunnies

INGREDIENTS

20 ripe plum tomatoes
¼ olive oil (use a silpat for oil free)
4-5 garlic cloves, finely chopped
S+P to taste

INSTRUCTIONS

1. Preheat oven to 375 degrees . Stem and slice in half lengthwise. Scoop out the seeds.

2. Lay tomatoes in a single layer on the baking sheet lined with a silpat mat. Drizzle with the olive oil and roast for 40 minutes. Increase the temperature to 400 degrees and roast about 20 minutes more.

ORANGE SPICED GRANOLA

Prep Time: 5 min | Total Time: 25 min | Serves: 8-10 Hungry Bunnies

INGREDIENTS

1 tsp cinnamon
½ tsp pink Himalayan salt
½ tsp coriander
½ tsp ginger
¼ tsp black pepper
⅛ tsp allspice
¼ tsp turmeric
¼ tsp cloves2 Tbs Olive oil
2 Tbs Maple syrup
½ of 1 Orange sliced
½ of 1 Orange juiced
¼ C Cashews
½ C Sliced almonds
¼ C Raisins
½ C Pecans
1½ C Steel cut oats

INSTRUCTIONS

1. Bake at 325 F. For 15-20 minutes, toss with more coconut sugar if you'd like. I personally like this recipe just the way it is!

SUN-DRIED TOMATO MAYO

Prep Time: 5 min | Total Time: 5 min | Serves: 6-8 Hungry Bunnies

INGREDIENTS

2-3 Tbs horseradish
1-2 Tbs spicy coarse ground mustard
½ C sun-dried tomatoes

INSTRUCTIONS

1. Whisk until thick and creamy.

RICOTTA CHEESE

Prep Time: 5 min | Total Time: 5 min | Serves: 10-13 Hungry Bunnies

INGREDIENTS

2 C raw cashews that soaked overnight
1 C unsweetened unflavored almond milk
3 Tbs fresh lemon or lime juice
4 Tbsp nutritional yeast
5 garlic cloves
2 tsp onion powder
2 tsp basil
1-2 tsp crushed red pepper (optional)
⅓ C fresh parsley (optional)
⅓ C fresh basil (optional)
5 sun dried tomatoes (optional)
Pink Himalayan salt to taste
1 tsp veggie pepper seasoning

INSTRUCTIONS

1. Add all ingredients into your Vitamix or high-speed blender and blend until thick and creamy.

FRENCH TOAST

Prep Time: 10 min | Total Time: 20 min | Serves: 3-5 Hungry Bunnies

INGREDIENTS

2 bananas
1 C almond milk or plant milk of choice
1 Tbs cinnamon
2 tsp vanilla
1 Tbs coconut sugar
⅛ tsp pink salt
⅛ tsp pepper (optional)
Bread of choice, I use Dave's Killer Bread

INSTRUCTIONS

1. Blend everything but the bread, then dip your bread and place immediately on a hot griddle. Cook 4-5 minutes on each side and serve with maple syrup!

BREAKFAST

ENGLISH BREAKFAST

Prep Time: 30 min | Total Time: 30 min | Serves: 3-5 Hungry Bunnies

INGREDIENTS

Sliced Tomato

Artichokes

Green Olives

Fresh Lemon to squeeze

Capers

Garlic toast (recipe for the bread can be found in my first book, Rabbit Food)

CHICKPEA SCRAMBLE

2 cans of chickpeas, rinsed and drained

2 tbsp lemon juice

2 tbsp Frontier Co-Op Organic Adobo Seasoning Blend

1/2-1 tsp turmeric powder

1/4 tsp Pink Himalayan salt

1 onion, diced small

INSTRUCTIONS

1. Add the chickpeas and the lemon juice to a mixing bowl and mash with a fork then add in the spices and mash again until well combined. Set aside while you sauté your onions.

2. Add the onions to a frying pan and sauté until golden brown. Add the chickpea scramble in a frying pan over medium-high heat for about 5 minutes or until golden brown, stirring occasionally. I personally only used a small amount of vegetable broth, no oil but you can use 1 Tbs of oil if you'd like.

3. I served my scramble with some lovely veggies, artichokes, capers, fresh lemon juice, potatoes, tomatoes and left over garlic toast. The recipe for the bread can be found in my cookbook, Rabbit Food and you can make it with white or wheat flour.

GOCHUGARU ROASTED POTATOES

Prep Time: 10 min | Total Time: 15-20 min

INGREDIENTS

4-5 Yukon gold potatoes, rinsed, peeled if desired, and cut into 2-inch chunks
Pink Himalayan salt to taste
1 Tbs Gochugaru Chili Pepper Flakes
1 Tbs Hungarian paprika
Parsley

INSTRUCTIONS

1. Preheat the oven to 500 degrees F. Cut the potatoes in half or quarters and place in a bowl with seasoning. Toss until the potatoes are well coated. Transfer the potatoes to a sheet pan, covered with a silpat mat and spread out into 1 layer.

2. Add salt to the water and bring to a boil over high heat. Reduce to a simmer, and cook until tender, about 5 minutes. Potatoes should show slight resistance when you poke them with a fork. Drain potatoes and transfer to a large bowl.

3. Toss the potatoes with seasoning, season with pepper and more salt to taste. Add the potatoes to a silpat covered baking sheet. Roast until bottoms of potatoes are crisp and golden brown, about 20 minutes total

4. If you need to, flip the potatoes and roast until second side is golden brown, another 15 to 20 minutes. Remove from the oven and set aside.

GAMJA JORIM

Prep Time: 5 min | Total Time: 10 min

INGREDIENTS

2 potatoes, washed, peeled, diced
1 onion, sliced
2 cloves garlic, crushed
1 Tbsp Gochujang
1 tsp Gochugaru
1 Tbsp date syrup

INSTRUCTIONS

1. Stir fry potatoes and onions in low sodium broth.

2. Add Gochujang, gochugaru, garlic, date syrup, and a little water. Cover and turn down heat. Cook until potatoes are tender.

MACA BLACKBERRY FREAKSHAKES

Prep Time: 10 min | Total Time: 10 min | Serves: 1-2 Hungry Bunnies

INGREDIENTS

BLACKBERRY NICE CREAM

2 Frozen sliced bananas, slice pieces before freezing
1 C frozen blackberries
2 Tbs coconut nectar
½ C nut milk for blending

BANANA MACA NICE CREAM

2 Frozen sliced bananas, slice pieces before freezing
1 tsp Vivo life maca powder
2 Tbs cinnamon, maca cashew butter
½ C nut milk for blending

TOPPINGS/LAYERING

Planet Protein peanut butter bar
Live Love Granola (or granola of choice)
Cinnamon (optional)
Pumpkin seeds
Cinnamon, maca cashew butter
Cacao nibs

INSTRUCTIONS

1. To your high speed blender or food processor add 2 frozen sliced bananas, & 1 tsp of Vivo life. Begin blending, slowly pour in the nut milk based on what your blender can handle. Add more if needed. Pour into a bowl & swirl in some nut butter of choice. I personally use cinnamon, maca cashew butter on the following page.

2. Repeat this process using the ingredients for the Blackberry nice cream. We make the banana Maca one first to avoid mixing any purple in!

3. Once you have both 'Nice' creams begin layering In your jar! I like to start with a layer of granola, but you can do whatever makes you happy!

CINNAMON MACA CASHEW BUTTER

Prep Time: 10 min | Total Time: 10 min | Serves: 8-10 Hungry Bunnies

INGREDIENTS

3 cup raw cashews

1 tsp vanilla bean powder

1/4 coconut sugar or coconut nectar

2 tsp melted coconut oil (optional, but adds to the "drippiness" factor)

6 tsp cinnamon *

2-3 tsp ground star anise *

6 tsp Vivo life maca

1/4 tsp sea salt

*Both of these can be optional or substituted with 3-4 tsp Chinese 5 spice

INSTRUCTIONS

1. In a high-powered blender, combine all of the ingredients above except for the maca and blend until creamy. You will likely need to scrape the sides occasionally. If you are using a Vitamix, you can use your tamper to assist with the blending.

2. Once the mixture is creamy, add the maca powder and blend until incorporated. This will thicken the butter slightly and if you prefer it to be more creamy then you may add in a bit more melted coconut oil.

3. Store in an air-tight container in a cool, dry place but not in the refrigerator! Enjoy!

DATE SYRUP

Prep Time: 5 min | Total Time: 5 min | Serves: 6-8 Hungry Bunnies

INGREDIENTS

9 medjool dates, pitted

1¼ C water, plus more for soaking dates

INSTRUCTIONS

1. Place the dates in a small bowl; cover with warm water and let sit for 30 minutes.

2. Once the dates have soaked, drain the water then add the dates, and fresh 1 ¼ water to the container of a high speed blender, such as a Vitamix.

3. Blend for 45-60 seconds, or until smooth. Transfer to an air tight container and store in the refrigerator for up to two weeks.

BREAKFAST BOWL *Magdalena*

Prep Time: 5 min | Total Time: 5 min | Serves: 1 Hungry Bunny

INGREDIENTS

6 Tbsp oats
1 Tbsp chia seeds
plant milk
1 ripe banana for sweetness
fruits of your choice (or other toppings)

INSTRUCTIONS

1. At first combine the oats of your choice, chia seeds, 1 sliced banana and plant milk Let it sit for about 10 minutes.

2. Now transfer everything into a small pot and let it cook until everything is super creamy and thick. (On low heat)

3. Don't forget to stir your porridge around constantly cause otherwise it'll stick to your pot.

4. For toppings you can use more fruit, chocolate, nuts, seeds or nut butters.

DELICIOUS VEGAN PANCAKES *Magdalena*

Prep Time: 5 min | Total Time: 15 min | Serves: 2-3 Hungry Bunnies

INGREDIENTS

¾ C-1 C spelt flour
2 ½ tsp vanilla sugar
1 ½ tsp baking powder
½ mashed banana
6-7 Tbs plant milk
2-3 Tbs sparkling water
sprinkle cinnamon
toppings of your choice

INSTRUCTIONS

1. Combine all of the dry ingredients in a bowl and mix until well incorporated, than add the wet ingredients.

2. After combining everything preheat a pan to medium high heat. Now let's make our pancakes! 1 pancake = 1 tablespoon of the dough.

3. As soon as there are bubbles on top of your pancakes you're ready to flip them over! (I promise that they won't stick to your pan.)

4. For toppings I used the other half of the banana, mango slices, peach slices, strawberries, cinnamon and dark chocolate.

CHICKPEA BREAKFAST HASH

Prep Time: 5 min | Total Time: 30 min | Serves: 5-7 Hungry Bunnies

INGREDIENTS

1 C garbanzo bean flour
½ tsp smoked alder salt
½ tsp baking powder
¾-1 C water
½-1 onion
2 Tbs veggie broth
1 Tbs arrowroot
1 tsp turmeric
1 tsp gochugaru Chile
1 tsp adobo
½ tsp black pepper

INSTRUCTIONS

1. In a large heated skillet, begin by sautéing onions and vegetable broth. I generally use enough vegetable broth to cover the onions. Season with smoked alder salt, pepper, and gochugaru.

2. Sauté until the liquid cooks down then add in whatever vegetables you'd like. I personally love adding tomatoes, zucchini , spinach and tomato. If you need to add more broth, feel free to do so.

3. In the meantime, add the garbanzo flour, smoked alder salt to taste, baking powder, arrowroot, turmeric, and more seasoning if you'd like. Blend the ingredients until smooth. Thank pour over the cooked veggies.

5. Allow the mixture to puff up a bit, almost like a pancake. Do not mix up the mixture until the batter really fluffs up, than scramble up and cook until desired. Serve with fresh veggies and spicy ketchup.

SPICY KETCHUP

Prep Time: 5 min | Total Time: 5 min

INGREDIENTS

½ C ketchup
½ C franks red hot

INSTRUCTIONS

1. Whisk until well incorporated.

BREAKFAST FRIENDLY BLISS BALLS *Sam Pickthall*

Prep Time: 15 min | Total Time: 15 min | Serves: 10-15 Hungry Bunnies

INGREDIENTS

1 C pitted dates, soaked in boiling water for 10 minutes
2 C rolled oats
¼ C hemp seeds, or chia seeds as an alternative
½ tsp ground cinnamon
½ C crunchy peanut butter, or almond butter as an alternative
2 Tbsp coconut oil, soft room temperature
2-3 Tbsp sesame seeds, for rolling

INSTRUCTIONS

1. Drain soaked dates and set aside.

2. Add all ingredients, except for the sesame seeds, to a high-speed food processor.

3. Process for 20-30 seconds or until mixture sticks together. Adding more coconut oil or peanut/almond butter, 1 tablespoon at a time, if needed to help the balls stick together and hold their shape.

4. Place the sesame seeds in a small bowl.

5. Pick up approx. 1-2 tablespoons of mixture and roll into balls.

6. Roll balls in sesame seeds and place in a Tupperware container that will be used to store the bliss balls. Repeat with remaining mixture.

7. Enjoy right away or refrigerate for 30 minutes until cold and firm. Serve and Enjoy!

CABBAGE SMOOTHIE

Prep Time: 5 min | Total Time: 5 min | Serves: 1 Hungry Bunny

INGREDIENTS

1 ½ C water
1 C blueberries, frozen
½ small head red cabbage, frozen
1 banana, frozen
1 grapefruit, peeled and seeded

INSTRUCTIONS

1. Break up the frozen cabbage and puree with water in a high speed blender.

2. Add frozen blueberries, banana and grapefruit and puree again until smooth.

ADAPTOGENIC SUPER FOODS CHIA PUDDING

Prep Time: 5 min | Total Time: 45 min | Serves: 6-8 Hungry Bunnies

INGREDIENTS

⅓ C date syrup
2 tsp raw vanilla bean
4 C plant milk
¾ C chia seeds
2-3 tsp four sigmatic super foods blend 10 mushroom blend

INSTRUCTIONS

1. In a bowl or mason jar, mix together all of the ingredients. If you're using a mason jar, you can put the lid on and shake the mixture to combine everything.

2. Whisk vigorously for 3 minutes. Refrigerate for 45 minutes or as long as overnight. Check on the pudding every so often and mix again so prevent everything from sinking to the bottom.

3. Lasts 3-5 days in the refrigerator.

CLEAR SKIN SMOOTHIE BOWL

Prep Time: 5 min | Total Time: 5 min | Serves: 2-3 Hungry Bunnies

INGREDIENTS

8 strawberries
1 C frozen fresh jackfruit
2 bananas
1/2 C grapefruit juice
1/2 C dark sweet cherries

INSTRUCTIONS

1. Blend all of the ingredients in a high speed blender, serve with hemp seeds, lime juice, kiwi, and whatever toppings you'd like!

APPLE HONEY GRANOLA

Prep Time: 5 min | Total Time: 5 min | Serves: 10 Hungry Bunnies

INGREDIENTS

4 C rolled oats
½ teaspoon salt
1 C walnuts
⅓ C coconut oil
⅔ C bee free apple honey
1 tsp almond extract

INSTRUCTIONS

1. Heat oven to 300 degrees. Combine oats, nuts, and salt in a large bowl and set aside. Combine oil, honey and almond extract in another, smaller bowl. Mix with your hands.

2. Spread the mixture onto two cookie sheets lined with a silpat mat. Bake 10 minutes. Then remove from oven and stir. Bake an additional 10 minutes or until slightly golden.

3. Remove from oven and allow to cool completely. When cooled, transfer into an airtight container for storage.

CHOCO CHAGA LOVE
BLISS BALLS *Monica Bozelle*

Prep Time: 5 min | Total Time: 5 min | Serves: 16-18 Hungry Bunnies

INGREDIENTS

16 pre-soaked dates (soak dates in a container for at least 1 hr.)

1 package of four sigmatic Chaga mushroom elixir

2 Tbs of unsweetened cacao or raw cocoa

½ C raw almonds

¼ C raw cashews (you can opt to use only almonds)

2-4 Tbs of unsweetened coconut flakes to roll balls with at the end before serving

INSTRUCTIONS

1. Place all ingredients in a food processor, make sure to scrape 2-3 times while pulsing ingredients to ensure everything is mixed well. It's okay to have some chunky nuts on the balls, this makes it extra yummy!

2. Make balls about 25-30 about the size of a cake-pop, follow by rolling your balls with coconut shreds on a large plate or cutting board.

3. Refrigerate & enjoy all week!

SPELT & CAROB PANCAKES

Prep Time: 5 min | Total Time: 20 min | Serves: 5-7 Hungry Bunnies

INGREDIENTS

1 ½ C spelt Flour
1½ Tbs baking powder
1½ C almond milk
3 Tbs agave
3 Tbs sunflower butter
1 Tbs carob syrup
⅛ tsp pink salt

INSTRUCTIONS

1. Mix the dry ingredients and then add the wet. Whisk until incorporated and then set aside.

2. Heat a large skillet or griddle and begin pouring in ½ C worth of pancake batter. Cook thoroughly and serve with fresh fruit.

BERRY COMPOTE

Prep Time: 5 min | Total Time: 5 min | Serves: 4 Hungry Bunnies

INGREDIENTS

¼ C coconut sugar
2 C strawberries, hulled, quartered
1 C blueberries
1 C blackberry
2 tsp fresh lemon juice
1 pinch pink salt

INSTRUCTIONS

1. In a large, sauté pan over medium heat, combine ¼ cup water & ¼ cup coconut sugar & bring to boil, stirring to dissolve sugar.

2. Cook 2 minutes, then add berries, lemon juice & salt.

3. Return to boil swirl mixture around in the pan, mash the berries to desired consistency.

4. Serve with pancakes or on top of desserts or ice cream.

LUNCH + BITES

GRAINS, GREENS & ROASTY THINGS

Prep Time: 30 min | Total Time: 1 hr 30 min

INGREDIENTS

Steamed mung beans
Steamed quinoa
Steamed Purple Cabbage
Steamed Corn
Steamed Kale
Buffalo tempeh
Tahini lemon vinaigrette
Marinated Mushrooms
Cinnamon sugar squash
Garlicky Swiss chard

INSTRUCTIONS

1. Steam your veggies, grains and beans according to packaging instructions and desired tenderness.

2. Prepare your Tahini lemon vinaigrette.

3. See recipes below for marinated mushrooms, cinnamon sugar squash and garlicky Swiss chard.

MARINATED MUSHROOMS

Prep Time: 10 min | Total Time: 25 min | Serves: 3-5 Hungry Bunnies

INGREDIENTS

½ C vegetable broth
2 pounds mushrooms, cleaned and quartered
2 lemons, zested and juiced
3 garlic cloves, sliced
2 bay leaves
½ C parsley
¼ C white wine vinegar or balsamic
¼ C diced red onion (optional)
Pink salt and freshly ground black pepper

INSTRUCTIONS

1. Add ¼ C vegetable broth to a large skillet over medium heat. Add the mushrooms and cook them for about 3 minutes.

2. Remove from the heat and stir in the lemon zest and juice, parsley, vinegar, onions, garlic, and bay leaves.

3. Pour over the remaining broth and season the mixture with salt and pepper. Pour into a bowl and allow to cool. Serve at room temperature.

CINNAMON SUGAR BUTTERNUT SQUASH

INGREDIENTS

2 large butternut squash, peeled, seeded and cut up
4 Tbs coconut sugar
1 ½ tsp ground cinnamon
Dash cayenne, optional
1 tsp smoked alder salt or pink salt

INSTRUCTIONS

1. Heat the oven to 425 F and line two large baking sheets with a silpat mat. Toss squash cubes with sugar, cinnamon, salt and the cayenne until well coated.

2. Add the coated squash onto baking sheets and spread into one layer. Try not to crowd them too much or else they will not brown.

3. Bake squash, turning about halfway through, until the centers are tender.

4. Bake for 40 to 45 minutes.

GARLICKY SWISS CHARD

Prep Time: 5 min | Total Time: 15 min

INGREDIENTS

2-3 heads of Swiss chard
1 head of roasted garlic
3-6 Tbs vegetable broth
½ tsp pink salt and pepper
1 Tbs adobo

INSTRUCTIONS

1. Heat the broth in heavy large pan over medium-low heat. Add garlic and seasoning. Sauté until fragrant, about 1 minute.

2. Add Swiss chard and stir to coat. Cover and cook until tender (stirring occasionally) about 8 minutes.

3. Taste and adjust seasoning as necessary.

TAHINI LEMON VINAIGRETTE

Prep Time: 5 min | Total Time: 5 min | Serves: 2-3 Hungry Bunnies

INGREDIENTS

½ C tahini.
⅔ to ¾ C water (as needed)
3 Tbs fresh lemon juice
1 clove garlic, minced
Dash of cayenne pepper (optional)
Pink salt and pepper to taste

INSTRUCTIONS

1. Whisk all ingredients together, the consistency will be up to you. You may choose to add more water according to how thin or thick you want this dressing to be. This will keep about 5 days in the refrigerator.

BUFFALO BLUE PIZZA

Prep Time: 10 min | Total Time: 30 | Serves: 4-6 Hungry Bunnies

INGREDIENTS

10 oz field roast 'Buffalo' wings
¼ C vegetable broth
Whole Foods whole grain pizza dough
Vegan blue cheese
Scallions
Persian cucumber
Fresh Basil

If you go to the pizza counter at whole foods you can ask for fresh whole grain pizza dough. This is a great option for a quick dinner.

INSTRUCTIONS

1. In a medium sized sauce pan, begin heating up the broth and add in the Buffalo wings and the sauce packet. I know that this is not according to the package instructions but I promise it is good.

2. Sauté the Buffalo wings, let them crumble and fall apart a bit. As they defrost chop them small with kitchen scissors and once they are defrosted turn off the gas and set aside.

3. Turn on your grill and set it to about 400 F. Spread out the pizza dough to desired size--this will be a more rustic type of pizza. Toss the pizza dough right on the hot grill and allow the dough to cook.

4. Add on your Buffalo wings, vegan blue cheese, scallions, cucumber, basil, red onion. If you would like more "buffalo sauce" add on some franks red hot.

BUFFALO SAUCE

Prep Time: 5 min | Total Time: 5 min

INGREDIENTS

1 C Franks red hot
1 C cashew cream

INSTRUCTIONS

1. Whisk together until well incorporated.

CREAMY DREAMY DILL DRESSING

Prep Time: 10 min | Total Time: 10 min | Serves: 5-7 Hungry Bunnies

INGREDIENTS

1 C cashew cream
1 tsp mustard powder
¼ C chickpeas
¼ tsp pink salt
1 Lemon Juiced
1 Tbs Hemp seeds
¼ C fresh dill
¼ C fresh parsley

INSTRUCTIONS

1. Take all of your ingredients and add them to your high speed blender. Blend until smooth & super creamy.

2. Add to your greens & top with whatever other veggies you'd like.

BERBERE CHICKPEAS

Prep Time: 5 min | Total Time: 5 min | Serves: 4 Hungry Bunnies

INGREDIENTS

2 cans of drained and rinsed chickpeas
1 Tbs avocado oil
1 Tbs Berbere seasoning
1 Tbs nutritional yeast
2 tsp garlic powder

INSTRUCTIONS

1. Preheat your oven to 450 F.

2. Toss your chickpeas in the seasoning and place them on a cookie sheet.

3. Allow the chickpeas to cook until crispy this can vary depending on your oven, roughly 30-40 minutes.

4. Remove from the hot oven, once they've finished cooking and set aside to cool.

KALE WALDORF SALAD *Julie Simone*

Prep Time: 5 min | Total Time: 30 min | Serves: 5-7 Hungry Bunnies

INGREDIENTS

One bunch kale
2 apples
2 celery stalks
½ lemon
¼ C Olive oil
3 tsp Dijon mustard
½ C Walnuts
½ C Raisins
Pinch Himalayan salt

INSTRUCTIONS

1. Wash and dry apples, kale and celery, set aside. Chop Kale into bite size pieces.

2. I personally prefer using kitchen shears. I find them super easy to use and get bite-size pieces rather quickly.

3. Combine Kale, juice from ¼ lemon, ⅛ C olive oil in a large bowl and massage using a kneading motion for several minutes until tender and reduced in size. If you want to make the kale tender and sweet and avoid jaw fatigue, you definitely want to massage it before combining the ingredients.

4. Chop Apples and celery into bite size pieces. Leave the skin on your apples to increase the fiber content of your dish

5. Break up the walnuts, since walnuts are a relatively soft nut, no fancy chopping cutlery here. Using just your hands you can easily break them apart in no time.

6. Whisk the remaining ⅛ C olive oil and ¼ C lemon juice with 3 tbsp Dijon mustard in a small bowl. Dijon mustard is the secret ingredient here that adds just the perfect dash of tang and spice. Add a bit more to up the spiciness.

7. Add apples and celery to the massaged kale. Add Dijon olive oil mixture to the kale mix and toss. Add the raisins and walnuts toss once more.

8. Salt and pepper to taste and serve

SUMMER POTATO SALAD

Prep Time: 10 min | Total Time: 40 min | Serves: 4-6 Hungry Bunnies

INGREDIENTS

2 pounds red new potatoes
1 pound of heirloom tomatoes or cherry
tomatoes, chopped small
1 Large onion, chopped small
1 Tbs fresh thyme leaves, chopped small
1 yellow bell pepper, chopped small
¼ C fresh basil, chopped small
¼ C fresh parsley, chopped small
⅛ C fresh oregano, chopped small
Pink salt and ground pepper

INSTRUCTIONS

1. Wash potatoes, cut them in half if small,
quartered if large. Add about one-inch of
water to the bottom of a large pot.

2. Place potatoes in the steamer basket.
Arranging the big potatoes on the bottom
of the basket and the little guys on top.
Cover and steam for about 30 minutes.

3. Check the potatoes, the tiny guys will
need to be checked after 20 minutes. For
big potatoes, wait 40 minutes. The potatoes
need to be fork tender, than drain and set
aside.

4. Toss everything together, if you'd like add
some red wine vinegar or balsamic.

AVOCADO VINAIGRETTE

Prep Time: 5 min | Total Time: 5 min

INGREDIENTS

1 avocado
½ C red wine vinegar

INSTRUCTIONS

1. Mash the avocado and then whisk
together until well incorporated.

'FRIED' HEARTS OF PALM CALAMARI

Prep Time: 10 min | Total Time: 30 min | Serves: 3-5 Hungry Bunnies

INGREDIENTS

CREAMY BATTER
1 C cashews soaked for 24 hours
2 C water (for soaking cashews)
1 sheet of toasted nori
½ tsp salt
black pepper to taste
1-2 tsp Korean Chile flakes

BREADING
1 C of millet flour
1 C polenta
1 Tbs old bay
Black pepper to taste
1 tsp Korean Chile flakes

INSTRUCTIONS

1. Get two 14 oz can of (Whole) hearts of palm cut them into pieces and remove the center.

2. Take the cashews plus the water they were soaking in and blend until a creamy batter forms. Add 1 sheet of toasted nori ½ tsp salt, black pepper to taste, 1-2 tsp, Korean Chile flakes then blend again.

3. Add the hearts of palm rings to the batter and prepare the breading.

4. Blend the millet flour, polenta, old bay, black pepper, Korean Chile flakes until a fine flour forms. Pour the batter soaked hearts of palm through a colander. Do this over a bowl to catch the excess liquid. Let the liquid drain so they are very lightly coated and not chunky.

5. Bread them with your hands, place on an oiled baking sheet or silpat mat. Continue until baking sheet is full.

6. Drizzle olive oil over top and place in the oven at 425 F. Maybe 6-10 minutes. I just watched them to be honest. Serve with cocktail sauce and fresh lemon!

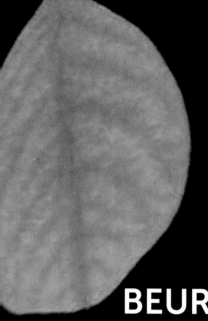

BEURRE BLANC SAUCE

Prep Time: 5 min | Total Time: 25 min

INGREDIENTS

1 C dry white wine
½ C white wine vinegar
1 shallot, finely chopped
1 Tbs lemon zest
1 lb. unsalted miyokos butter, cold
¼ C cashew cream
⅛ teaspoon white pepper, or to taste
Pink salt, to taste

INSTRUCTIONS

1. Boil wine, vinegar, and shallot in a saucepan over medium heat until liquid thickens and reduces--about 5 minutes. Add cashew cream, pink salt, and white pepper and bring to a boil, 1 minute.

2. Reduce the heat to low and add a 2 Tbs butter, whisking constantly. Add remaining butter a few pieces at a time, whisking constantly. Continue adding the butter cubes until they are all melted.

3. Remove the sauce from heat, then season to taste with salt and pepper. Emulsify with an immersion blender.

COCKTAIL SAUCE

Prep Time: 5 min | Total Time: 5 min | Serves: 10-12 Hungry Bunnies

INGREDIENTS

2 C ketchup
1 Tbs Worcestershire sauce
1 Tbs lemon juice + 1 Tbs zest
2 tsp horseradish adjust to taste
1 tsp hot sauce

INSTRUCTIONS

1. Stir all ingredients together in a small bowl until combined.

LEMON AIOLI

Prep Time: 5 min | Total Time: 5 min | Serves: 3-4 Hungry Bunnies

INGREDIENTS

½ C mayo
1 tsp finely grated lemon zest
1- 1½ Tbs fresh lemon juice
1 clove garlic, minced
1 teaspoon Dijon mustard
Pink salt and pepper to taste
¼ C fresh basil, chopped small
¼ C fresh parsley, chopped small

INSTRUCTIONS

1. Blend the mayo, lemon zest, lemon juice, garlic clove, Dijon, pink salt and pepper together

2. Mix in the herbs and enjoy!

BAKED BUFFALO TEMPEH

Prep Time: 20 min | Total Time: Overnight | Serves: 4-8 Hungry Bunnies

INGREDIENTS

3 8oz packs of tempeh
2 C Franks Red Hot
2 C Unsweetened Plant Milk
2 Tbs Frontier Co-Op Organic Adobo
Seasoning Blend

Adjust the amount of cashew cream according to how mild, or how spicy you'd like these to be. Use ½ C for more heat and use 1 C for more medium.

INSTRUCTIONS

1. To remove bitterness from the tempeh, bring a saucepan filled with 1 inch of water to a low boil over medium heat. Steam tempeh for a total of 10, flipping once at the halfway point.

2. Rinse, pat dry, and slice the tempeh in half lengthwise then cutting into small triangles. The smaller the pieces, the better they can soak up the marinade. Set aside while you create your marinade.

3. Mix marinade by adding Franks Red Hot as well as Plant milk to a bowl. Whisk together until incorporated. Add in your seasoning, and adjust to your liking.

4. Add the sliced tempeh to the marinade and toss to coat. Then cover and refrigerate for at least 3 hours, but this works best if you marinade overnight. 24 hours definitely infuses the most flavor!

5. While marinating, toss/stir occasionally to ensure even coating. (Just before baking, drizzle with additional sauce)

6. Once marinated, preheat oven to 375 F. and line a baking sheet with parchment paper or a silpat mat. Add tempeh and reserve any leftover marinade to brush/coat the tempeh once baked. Bake for 30 minutes. Remove from oven and brush/coat with any remaining marinade.

PEA & GARLIC PESTO BAKED TEMPEH

Prep Time: 15 minutes | Total Baking Time: overnight

INGREDIENTS

TEMPEH

32 oz Tempeh, cut into triangles
2 Tbsp vegetable broth
½ Tbsp smoked alder salt
1 tsp black pepper

MARINADE/GLAZE

1 C refrigerated pesto
¼ C rawmesan (vegan Parmesan)

TOPPING

Crushed red pepper

INSTRUCTIONS

1. Marinade the tempeh overnight in vegetable broth, smoked alder salt, pepper and ½ C pesto.

2. When you are ready to bake position a rack in the top of the oven than preheat to 400 F. Line a baking sheet with a silpat mat in order to prevent from using oil.

3. Bake for 15 minutes, than flip, brush with the remaining pesto and bake for an additional 15 minutes. Once the tempeh is finished baking toss it in a bowl with the rawmesan cheese.

PEA & GARLIC PESTO

Prep Time: 5 min | Total Time: 5 min

INGREDIENTS

½ C steamed peas
2 C spinach
2 sprigs of fresh oregano
½ C fresh basil
½ C fresh parsley
2 cloves of fresh garlic
2 Tbs of capers (stirred in)

INSTRUCTIONS

1. Add all the ingredients for the pesto to your food processor and blend until well incorporated.

2. You may add olive oil according to preference, I personally don't use any for this recipe.

RAWMESAN

Prep Time: 5 min | Total Time: 5 min | Serves: 5-7 Hungry Bunnies

INGREDIENTS

1 C raw cashews
4 Tbsp nutritional yeast
¾ tsp pink salt

INSTRUCTIONS

1. Add all ingredients to a food processor and blend until powdery. If you keep this in the refrigerator it will last up to 20 days.

BUFFALO CAULIFLOWER BITES

Prep Time: 10 min | Total Time: 30 | Serves: 4-6 Hungry Bunnies

INGREDIENTS

1 head of cauliflower
½ C of almond flour (or regular flour)
½-1 C of almond milk
2 tsp of garlic powder
Salt and pepper to taste
⅔-1 C franks red hot
2-3 Tbs cashew cream

INSTRUCTIONS

1. Preheat the oven to 450 F. Chop your cauliflower into pieces, rinse dry and set aside. In a bowl whisk together the flour, almond milk, garlic powder, salt and pepper.

2. Combine it with the cauliflower with the mixture you just created and then place on a baking sheet. You are going to want to apply some olive oil or a silpat mat to prevent the cauliflower from sticking.

3. Bake for 15 minutes tossing occasionally. In the meantime whisk together cashew cream, Frank's red hot and an additional splash of milk--about 2 Tbs this is optional, but prevents them from being too spicy.

4. Once your Cauliflower is finished cooking remove it from the oven and cover with the sauce that you just made. Place the cauliflower back in the oven and cook it for an additional 30-35 minutes tossing occasionally. If you want this to be a little extra crispy then you are going to want to cook them with olive oil!

OVEN ROASTED POTATOES WITH BBQ SEASONING

Prep Time: 10 min | Total Time: 45 | Serves: 4-6 Hungry Bunnies

INGREDIENTS

4 ½ pounds red potatoes, rinsed, peeled if desired, cut into chunks
2-3 Tbs BBQ seasoning

INSTRUCTIONS

1. Adjust oven racks to lower and upper positions. Preheat oven to 500 F. Place potatoes in a large pot and cover with cold water.

2. Bring to a boil over high heat, reduce to a simmer, and cook until fork tender. Potatoes should show slight resistance. Drain potatoes and transfer to a large bowl.

3. Season with BBQ seasoning to taste than divide potatoes evenly between 2 baking sheets lined with a silpat mat.

4. Transfer baking sheets to oven and roast until potatoes are crisp, about 20 minutes total, swapping trays top for bottom and rotating them once halfway through roasting. Toss and bake for an additional 15 minutes or until desired crispness.

BBQ SEASONING

Prep Time: 5 min | Total Time: 5 min

INGREDIENTS

½ tsp Celery Salt
1 tsp cayenne
2 tsp turmeric
½ Tbs Black Pepper
1 Tbs ancho chili powder
1 Tbs garlic powder + 1 Tbs onion powder
1 Tbs Parsley
2 Tbs Dried Mustard
¼ C Tbs Smoked Paprika
¼ C coconut sugar

INSTRUCTIONS

1. Mix together until well incorporated.

BBQ CAULIFLOWER BITES

Prep Time: 10 min | Total Time: 45 | Serves: 4-6 Hungry Bunnies

INGREDIENTS

1 head of cauliflower
½ C of almond flour (or regular flour)
½-1C of water or almond milk
2 tsp of garlic powder
Salt and pepper to taste
2-3 Tbs cashew cream
2/3-1 C BBQ sauce

INSTRUCTIONS

1. Preheat the oven to 450 F. Chop up your cauliflower into pieces, rinse, dry and set aside. In a bowl whisk together the flour, liquid, garlic powder, salt and pepper.

2. Combine the cauliflower with the mixture you just created and then place on a baking sheet. You are going to want to apply some olive oil or a silpat mat to prevent the cauliflower from sticking.

3. Bake for 15 minutes tossing occasionally. In the meantime whisk together cashew cream and BBQ sauce.

4. Once your Cauliflower is done cooking remove it from the oven and cover with the sauce that you just made. Place the cauliflower back in the oven and cook it for an additional 30-35 minutes tossing occasionally. If you want this to be a little extra crispy then you are going to want to cook them with olive oil!

BURGERS + SANDWICHES

BUFFALO TEMPEH SANDWICH

Prep Time: 10 min | Total Time: 10 | Serves: 1 Hungry Bunny

INGREDIENTS

Buffalo tempeh
Red cabbage
Tomato
Persian cucumber
Arugula
Sun dried tomato mayo
Sliced bread of choice

INSTRUCTIONS

1. Assemble your sandwich according to your preferences. Add whatever else you'd like.

SUN DRIED TOMATO MAYO

Prep Time: 5 min | Total Time: 5 min | Serves: 8-10 Hungry Bunnies

INGREDIENTS

1 C mayonnaise
¼ C chopped sun-dried tomatoes
2 tsp fresh lemon juice
¼ C fresh basil
¼ C fresh parsley
Black pepper to taste

INSTRUCTIONS

1. In a food processor, blend 1 C mayonnaise, 1/4 cup chopped sun-dried tomatoes and 2 tsp. fresh lemon juice, basil, parsley, pepper.

THE NASTY PATTY

Prep Time: 10 min | Total Time: 10 | Serves: 1 Hungry Bunny

INGREDIENTS

FOR THE BURGER

1 L onion, diced small
7 cloves of garlic, diced small
½ of a head of celery, chopped as small as possible
1 Tbs adobo seasoning
1 C peas
1 C kale
1 C broccoli
1 can of cannellini beans
2 C of oats (1 c for blending 1 c for mixing)
1 C sun dried tomatoes
2 Tbs Worcestershire sauce
2 Tbs green Chiles
1 tsp liquid smoke
Fresh basil and parsley optional and to taste

TOPPINGS

Eggplant bacon
Thousand island dressing
Mustard
Kale
Spicy Ketchup
Tomato
Red onion
Whole grain bun
Daiya cheddar cheese

INSTRUCTIONS

1. Pan fry the onions, garlic and celery in 2 Tbs of avocado oil or 1 Tbs of low sodium veggie broth until transparent, fragrant and caramelized. Season with 1 Tbs of adobo seasoning or to taste, place in a bowl and set aside.

2. Steam your veggies and set aside. In a food processor puree the rinsed and drained beans, sun-dried tomatoes (removed from the oil, or water) Worcestershire, green Chiles, liquid smoke, herbs, and 1 C worth of oats. When the mixture is combined and smooth add it to the same bowl with the onions and garlic.

3. Return to your food processor and add in the steamed veggies, pulse until crumbly, you don't want them to be pureed otherwise you will lose the texture of these burgers.

4. Transfer to that same bowl and add in the remainder of the oats. Begin to combine the mixture with your hands. Taste and see if more salt and pepper is needed. Refrigerate the mixture for 1 hour.

5. Form 5-6 patties and pan fry them in a small amount of avocado oil. This should take about 5 minutes on each side, covering with a lid on the second side to ensure the patties cook through a bit. You want the outside to have a little bit of a crisp.

6. (Optional) Bake at 350 F. for 10 minutes, flipping in between. You may bake these longer but I liked that they still had a softness to them.

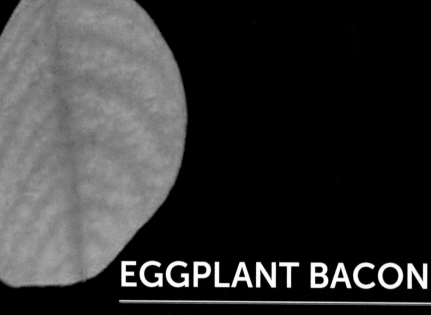

EGGPLANT BACON

Prep Time: 10 min | Total Time: 60 min

INGREDIENTS

1 medium eggplant
2 Tbsp avocado oil
½ Tbsp coconut nectar
1 Tbs coconut sugar
2 Tbsp vegan Worcestershire
1 Tbs molasses
3 tsp liquid smoke
1 tsp paprika
1/2 tsp black pepper
1 tsp BBQ seasoning

INSTRUCTIONS

1. Preheat oven to 300 F and line a baking sheet with a silpat mat.

2. Slice an eggplant into very thin strips, using a sharp knife or mandolin.

3. Brush on the sauce mixture and arrange the eggplant strips on your baking sheet in one single layer.

4. Bake until eggplant is cooked through and beginning to get crisp, 45-50 minutes.

THOUSAND ISLAND

Prep Time: 5 min | Total Time: 5 min

INGREDIENTS

2-4 Tbs pickle juice

1 dill pickle, diced small

½ C vegan mayo

3-6 Tbs organic ketchup

½-1 Tbs horseradish

½-1 Tbs spicy brown mustard (optional)

INSTRUCTIONS

1. Add all of your ingredients to a bowl, whisk until smooth and creamy.

SPINACH & PARSLEY POTATO CROQUETTES

Prep Time: 10 min | Total Time: 60 min | Serves: 8-10 Hungry Bunnies

INGREDIENTS

2 Tbs Plant milk
½ tsp pepper + ½ tsp pink salt
1 tsp chopped green onion
3 Tbs spelt flour
4 C mashed potatoes
1 flax egg
1 C suateed spinach, chopped small
¼ C parsley, chopped small
Dried bread crumbs

INSTRUCTIONS

1. Add plant milk, flour, salt, pepper, chopped green onion, and flax egg to mashed potatoes.

2. Preheat your oven to 400 F. while you're mixture chills in the fridge for about 30 minutes. Then shape them into patties or little logs, dip them in flax egg, and roll them through bread crumbs before placing them into the oven.

3. Bake on a silpat mat at 400 F. Cook until crispy and golden, about 25 minutes.

LENTIL PATTIES

Prep Time: 20 min | Total Time: 60 min | Serves: 10-12 Hungry Bunnies

INGREDIENTS

1 C dry lentils, sorted and well rinsed

2 ½ C water or vegetable broth

1 bay leaf

2 Tbs vegetable broth

1 onion, diced small

1 carrot, shredded

2 stalks of celery

1 Tbs Worcestershire sauce

¾ C oat flour

¾ C breadcrumbs

½ tsp salt + 1 tsp pepper

INSTRUCTIONS

1. Boil the lentils according to the packaging instructions, toss in a bay leaf, live a little. Lentils will be soft and most of the water will be gone.

2. Preheat the oven to 400 F. Cook the onions, celery and carrot in the broth until soft, about 5 minutes.

3. In a bowl mix the cooked ingredients with the pepper, Worcestershire sauce, oats and bread crumbs.

4. While still warm form the mixture into patties, this makes 8-10 burgers.

5. Bake on a silpat mat at 400 F. for 15-20 minutes.

GREEN MONSTER PATTY

Prep Time: 20 min | Total Time: 60 min | Serves: 5-7 Hungry Bunnies

INGREDIENTS

1 L onion, sautéed
7 garlic cloves, sautéed
1 C oats
2-3 Tbs bread crumbs
2 Tbs pesto
1 Tbs adobo
1 C oat flour
1 C chickpeas
½ C steamed broccoli
¼ C parsley
2 Tbs Worcestershire sauce
1 C walnuts
1 ½ tsp liquid smoke
½ C peas

INSTRUCTIONS

1. Begin by adding your sautéed onions, sautéed garlic, 1 C of oats, 2 Tbs bread crumbs, 2 Tbs pesto to a large bowl. Mix and set aside.

2. Add 1 Tbs adobo, 1 C oat flour, 1 C chickpeas, ½ C steamed broccoli, ¼ C parsley, 2 Tbs, Worcestershire sauce, 1 C walnuts, 1 ½ tsp, liquid smoke, ½ C peas to your food processor. Pulse until crumbly, not smooth.

3. Add half of that crumbly mixture to a bowl and then puree the remaining half. Add that to the bowl, along with everything else and mix using your hands.

4. Once everything is well incorporated, place the bowl in the fridge for about 30 minutes to an hour so. You want the mixture to become more dense, this is ideal for forming patties.

5. Form patties and pan fry them in a small amount of avocado oil. This should take about 5 minutes on each side, covering with a lid on the second side to ensure the patties cook through a bit. You want the outside to have a little bit of a crisp.

6. (Optional) Bake at 350 F. for 10 minutes, flipping in between. You may bake these longer but I liked that they still had a softness to them.

EGGPLANT MEATBALL SUB

Prep Time: 20 min | Total Time: 70 min | Serves: 5-7 Hungry Bunnies

INGREDIENTS

1 Large eggplant
6-8 cloves of roasted garlic
1 Large onion
¾ C raisins
1- 1 ½ Tbs olive oil + 1 Tbs (for drizzling)
1 ½ C GF breadcrumbs
1 tsp oregano
1 C carrot
2 Tbs balsamic (optional)
½ C fresh parsley
Salt & Pepper to taste

INSTRUCTIONS

1. Preheat your oven to 400 F. Peel & chop up your eggplant, onion, garlic, & carrots.

2. Put them on a cookie sheet & drizzle on some olive oil, oregano salt & pepper. Place them in the oven & allow them to roast for 30 minutes, tossing & adding balsamic about halfway through.

3. When 30 minutes hits, decrease your oven to 350 F. let them roast for 10 more minutes. Remove from the oven & add to a food processor.

4. Add the bread crumbs, & parsley. Pulse until the mixture is combined & mailable. Remove the mixture & add to a bowl, adding in your raisins & mixing with your hands.

5. Form patties & place them back onto the cookie sheet. Bake on a silpat mat to prevent from sticking & place them into the oven to cook for 30 minutes until they begin to crisp up.

6. Serve with vegan mozzarella cheese on your favorite roll with some fresh basil.

PINEAPPLE BBQ JACKFRUIT

Prep Time: 5 min | Total Time: 40 min | Serves: 4-6 Hungry Bunnies

INGREDIENTS

½ red onion
4-6 cloves of garlic
¼ C pineapple juice
¼ C chopped pineapple
1 C veggie broth
2 tsp liquid smoke
1 tsp nutmeg
1 tsp Cajun seasoning
1 tsp paprika
1 C BBQ sauce

INSTRUCTIONS

1. Blend everything, except for the jackfruit, in the blender, then pour into a large heated skillet. Add in the 1 kg or 4-5 C of rinsed & drained jackfruit.

2. Allow the mixture to come to a boil then reduce to a simmer & cook for roughly 20-30 minutes.

3. For the sauce I mixed 1 C my homemade vegan mayo (recipe in my book) with 1-2 Tbs of franks red hot.

4. Add 2 Tbs of pineapple juice & the juice of ½ a lime. Whisk & set aside.

5. Once the jackfruit is prepared add it to your burger bun. Top with raw slaw or coleslaw, orange chipotle mayo, grilled pineapple and pickled tomatoes.

PEPPERS ONIONS & POTATOES

Prep Time: 20 min | Total Time: 50 min | Serves: 4-6 Hungry Bunnies

INGREDIENTS

1 Tbs olive oil or vegetable broth

4 large potatoes peeled and thickly sliced

4 large red bell peppers, seeded and cut into wedges

3 large onions, cut into wedges

½ C white wine

½ C vegetable broth

1 tsp Italian seasoning

1 tsp adobo

¼ C fresh basil

1-2 C tomato sauce, jarred or fresh

*Seitan cutlet recipe not provided, this was a spontaneous recipe test and will be added to my website upon completion

INSTRUCTIONS

1. Preheat oven to 400 degrees F. Heat 2 tsp olive oil (or vegetable broth for oil free) in a pan over medium heat.

2. Cook the potatoes, stirring occasionally, until browned, about 10 minutes. Place the potatoes into the baking dish. Add the red peppers and onions to the hot skillet and cook until they are beginning to soften, about 5 minutes.

3. Add the vegetables to the baking dish. Pour wine, sauce and broth over the vegetables.

4. Sprinkle on the herbs and seasoning, salt, and pepper. Gently stir everything together and then bake in the preheated oven until hot and bubbling, 20 to 25 minutes.

5. Check them and see if they are fork tender, if they need to cook longer then let them cook for an additional 15-20 minutes.

6. Serve on a roll with mustard, and a seitan cutlet. (Optional)

QUINOA CHICKPEA BURGER

Prep Time: 15 min | Total Time: 50 min | Serves: 5-7 Hungry Bunnies

INGREDIENTS

1 L onion, sautéed
7 garlic cloves, sautéed
1 C oats
1- 1 ½ C cooked quinoa
½ broccoli
2 Tbs tahini
¼ C parsley
1 can chickpeas
2 Tbs adobo
1 C oat flour
2 Tbs Worcestershire sauce
2 ½ tsp liquid smoke
1 C sun dried tomatoes

INSTRUCTIONS

1. Begin by adding your sautéed onions, sautéed garlic, 1 C of oats, cooked quinoa. Mix and then set to the side.

2. In your food processor, add ½ broccoli, 2 Tbs tahini, ¼ C parsley, 1 can chickpeas, 2 Tbs adobo, 1 C oat flour, 2 Tbs, Worcestershire sauce, 2 ½ tsp liquid smoke, 1 C sun dried tomatoes. Pulse until crumbly, not smooth.

3. Add half of that crumbly mixture to a bowl and then puree the remaining half. Add that to the bowl, along with everything else and mix using your hands.

4. Once everything is well incorporated, place the bowl in the fridge for about 30 minutes to an hour so. You want the mixture to become more dense, this is ideal for forming patties.

5. Form patties and pan fry them in a small amount of avocado oil. This should take about 5 minutes on each side, covering with a lid on the second side to ensure the patties cook through a bit. You want the outside to have a little bit of a crisp.

6. (Optional) Bake at 350 F. for 10 minutes, flipping in between. You may bake these longer but I liked that they still had a softness to them.

RAINBOW SANDWICH

Prep Time: 5 min | Total Time: 10 min | Serves: 1 Hungry Bunnies

INGREDIENTS

Beet and spirulina colored cashew mayo
Kale
Pepperoncini pepper
Cucumber
Sunflower sprouts
Tomato
Lemon
Carrot
Mango habanero silly chilly hot sauce
Purple cabbage
Fresh dill
Basil
Bread of choice

INSTRUCTIONS

1. Begin by mixing a small amount of spirulina and a splash of beet juice into the cashew mayo, or vegan mayo of choice.

2. Pile sandwich high and enjoy.

SOUP + STEW

FORBIDDEN RICE NOODLE SOUP

Prep Time: 15 min | Total Time: 6 hours | Serves: 8-10 Hungry Bunnies

INGREDIENTS

1 L yellow onion diced small

6-8 garlic cloves

1 L thumb of ginger

2 Tbs sesame oil (I used spicy sesame oil)

1 entire head of Celery chopped small

4 L carrots chopped small

1 L head of Savoy cabbage

1 Tbs mellow white miso

1 Tbs Korean Chile flakes

2 pureed red belle peppers

2-4 Tbs liquid aminos (or soy sauce)

12-18 C water

INSTRUCTIONS

1. Puree the garlic & the ginger. Add to a hot skillet with 2 Tbs of sesame oil, ¼ tsp pink salt, ¼ tsp black pepper. Sauté until garlic is fragrant. Add in the carrots & the celery.

2. Add in your chopped Savoy cabbage, 1 Tbs of mellow white miso, 1 Tbs of Korean Chile flakes, 2 pureed belle peppers, 2-4 Tbs liquid aminos.

3. Mix everything & then cover with water, I personally was using a massive pot & I added between 12-18 C but you want to be sure the vegetables are submerged & that there is enough liquid in the pot. You may use vegetable broth but the beauty of this soup is the broth that forms from cooking for a long time.

4. Let everything come to a boil, then reduce to simmer. Cook for 4-6 hours if using water, with the lid tilted.

5. Serve with black forbidden rice noodles, fresh lemon, liquid aminos, pickled jalapeños, kimchi & more Korean Chile flakes

BEATRIX POTTER SPLIT PEA STEW

Prep Time: 5 min | Total Time: 70 min | Serves: 8-10 Hungry Bunnies

INGREDIENTS

16 oz green split peas
Water
1 L head of celery, grated
4-5 juicing carrots, grated
1 L onion, grated
3-5 cloves of garlic chopped small
2 bay leafs
scallions for topping
radishes for topping
hot sauce for serving
lemon for serving

INSTRUCTIONS

1. Prepare the split peas according to packaging instructions. I cooked mine in water.

2. While they are cooking, add in all of the chopped vegetables and the bay leaves.

3. Allow everything to cook until the split peas are soft.

4. I know this recipe is pretty simple but i promise the simplicity makes it delicious.

PURPLEY PURPLE SOUP

Prep Time: 10 min | Total Time: 3 hours | Serves: 8-10 Hungry Bunnies

INGREDIENTS

2 L red onions, chopped
2 red apples, chopped
½ head of celery, chopped
1 small head of fennel, chopped
1 small leek, chopped
1 purple cabbage, chopped
5 C veggie broth
¼ C basil
1 Tbs adobo
1 can coconut milk
splash of balsamic
sun dried tomatoes for serving
sprouts for serving
scallions for serving

INSTRUCTIONS

1. To a large stock pot add 2 L red onions, chopped, ½ head of celery, 1 small head of fennel, 2 red apples, 1 small leek, 1 purple cabbage.

2. Pour in some broth. Steam and sauté until soft, allowing everything to cook down.

3. Add in the broth, adobo, basil, coconut milk and balsamic. Let everything come to a boil, then reduce to a simmer.

4. Simmer for 10-15 minutes., Then you are going to transfer the soup to a blender and blend it until smooth.

5. Serve with additional coconut milk, scallions, sprouts, sun dried tomatoes, and sprouts.

THE BEST DAMN CURRY EVER *Kemal*

Prep Time: 10 min | Total Time: 30 min

INGREDIENTS

1 Tbsp coconut oil
1 white onion
2 Tbsp garlic
2 Tbsp curry powder
Thumb of minced ginger
2 Tbsp tomato paste
2 Tbsp liquid amino braggs (soy/tamari)
3 Tbsp maple syrup
1 C canned coconut milk full fat
2 C veg broth
1 lb Yukon gold potatoes chopped finely
4 carrots chopped finely
1 cauliflower chopped finely
1 can of chickpeas
1 bunch of fresh cilantro

INSTRUCTIONS

1. Cook your onion down in coconut oil for 5 minutes then add garlic & minced ginger

2. Add your tomato paste, soy, maple syrup, and curry powder, cook 2 minutes

3. Add your veg broth, the full 2 cups, now add your chopped potato and carrots

4. Cook for 7 minutes with the lid cracked open for ventilation on medium heat

5. Remove lid and add chickpeas, coconut milk & chopped cauliflower, reduce heat a little here

6. Cook for another 5-7 minutes, fold in your chopped cilantro and serve over rice of choice!

YELLOW LENTIL SOUP

Prep Time: 10 min | Total Time: 40 min | Serves: 6-8 Hungry Bunnies

INGREDIENTS

3 Tbs vegetable broth, for sautéing

1 L yellow onion, chopped

2-3 tsp grated ginger

2 cloves garlic, minced

2 tsp gochugaru Chile

1 tsp coriander

½ tsp turmeric

¼ tsp coriander

1 tsp pink salt

1½ C yellow lentils, sorted and rinsed

2 C low-sodium vegetable broth

2 Tbs pureed roasted red pepper

INSTRUCTIONS

1. Heat the broth in a saucepan over medium-high heat. Stir in the onions, garlic and seasonings, and sauté 1 minute.

2. Add lentils, vegetable broth, 2 cups water, and turmeric. Cover, reduce heat to medium-low, and simmer 25 minutes, or until liquid is absorbed.

3. Add in the ginger and stir in the pureed roasted red pepper. Simmer for an additional 10-15 minutes and then turn off the gas.

4. Transfer to a blender and puree the mixture, this step is optional.

5. Serve with lime juice, roasted red peppers, sprouts, radishes and ginger.

BEET BROTH
HOT & SOUR SOUP

Prep Time: 10 min | Total Time: 40 min | Serves: 6-8 Hungry Bunnies

INGREDIENTS

3 Tbs vegetable broth, for sautéing
1 Tbs grated ginger
4 cloves garlic, minced
1 beet sliced
1 L yellow onion, chopped
7½ C vegetable broth
2 tsp Gochugaru Chili Pepper Flakes
8 oz of mushrooms
½ C beet juice
2-3 Tbs rice vinegar
2 Tbs Gochujang Fermented Chili
1 Tbs liquid aminos
2 Tbs arrowroot mixed with ¼ C cold water
scallions for serving
Lime juice for serving
Lotus foods rice noodles

INSTRUCTIONS

1. Heat the broth in a large saucepan over medium heat. Add ginger and garlic and carefully sauté for about one minute.

2. Add broth, and the sliced beet, raise the heat, and bring the mixture to a boil.

3. Reduce to a simmer and add mushrooms, and simmer for about ten minutes.

4. Stir in the vinegar, chili paste, beet juice and liquid aminos. Simmer an additional ten minutes then taste and adjust the seasonings to your liking.

5. Add the cornstarch mixture into the broth, stir well, and remove from heat.

6. Prepare your noodles and serve with fresh lime juice and scallions.

FEAST

ENCHILADAS

Prep Time: 40 min | Total Time: 70 min | Serves: 5-7 Hungry Bunnies

INGREDIENTS

¼ C vegetable broth

1 onion

5 garlic cloves

2 roasted poblano, diced

½ C sun dried tomato paste

1 kg jackfruit

2 C spinach

2½ C enchilada sauce

1 Tbs lime juice

1 tsp chili powder

1 tsp cumin

½ tsp pink salt

5-6 Coconut Flour Tortillas by The Real Coconut Co.

4 oz green Chiles, medium heat

2½ C Homemade Enchilada Sauce

INSTRUCTIONS

1. Preheat the oven to 350 F. Prepare a large rectangular baking dish by applying some avocado oil to prevent sticking, set aside.

2. In a large skillet, sauté onions and garlic and over medium heat until the onion softens. Season with salt and pepper.

3. Add the roasted poblano peppers, sun-dried tomato paste and jackfruit. Cook for 10 to 15 minutes over medium-high heat, and then add the spinach. Cook until it is wilted.

4. Stir in ½ C enchilada sauce. Than add the lime juice, chili powder, cumin, and salt. Taste and adjust seasonings.

5. Add ¼-½ C of Enchilada Sauce onto the bottom of your casserole dish and spread it out evenly.

6. Scoop some of the filling onto each tortilla than roll it and place it, seam side down, in the casserole dish. Spread the leftover filling, on top of the tortillas.

7. Pour the remaining enchilada sauce on top of the tortillas until they are completely covered in sauce.

8. Bake the enchiladas, uncovered, at 350 F for 20 to 25 minutes, until the sauce is a deep red color and the enchiladas are heated through.

9. Serve with lime Chile sauce, cashew sour cream, diced peppers and tomatoes, sprouts, and guacamole.

ENCHILADA SAUCE

Prep Time: 5 minutes | Total Time: 15

INGREDIENTS

4¼ C vegetable broth
2 Tbs spelt flour
2½ Tbs chili powder
1½ tsp roasted garlic, diced small
1½ tsp cumin
1½ tsp onion powder
¼-½ tsp cayenne
1½ C sun dried tomato paste
28 oz veggie broth
½-1 tsp pink salt

*Recipe inspired by Angelo, Oh She Glows

INSTRUCTIONS

1. Heat the ¼ C vegetable broth at medium heat and begin to whisk in the spelt flour to form a roux or paste. Stir in the chili powder, garlic powder, cumin, onion powder, and cayenne pepper until combined.

2. Cook for a couple minutes over medium heat until fragrant. Add in sun dried tomato paste and 4 C of vegetable broth. Whisk until smooth.

3. Bring to a simmer over low heat. Taste and adjust seasoning and then continue simmering until thickened.

SUN DRIED TOMATO PASTE

Prep Time: 10 min | Total Time: 40 min | Serves: 5-7 Hungry Bunnies

INGREDIENTS

1 yellow onion, thinly sliced
3 cloves of roasted garlic peeled, minced
2 C sun-dried tomatoes with herbs in oil drained, oil reserved
1½ C water
¼ cup red wine vinegar
½ tsp black pepper
½-1 Tbs balsamic vinegar

INSTRUCTIONS

1. Heat the 1 Tbsp of the reserved sun-dried tomato oil in a skillet and add the onions and garlic. Cook them, until the onions begin to soften.

2. Add the sun-dried tomatoes, water, red wine vinegar, salt, and pepper to the pan

3. Bring to a boil, then reduce it to low and let it simmer for 30 minutes.

Remove from the heat, and let the mixture cool completely.

4. Add the contents to a blender and pulse until thick, spreadable paste that still has good texture.

5. Use within 2 weeks.

LIME CHILE SAUCE

Prep Time: 10 min | Total Time: 10 min

INGREDIENTS

1 C cashews, soaked overnight
½ C chickpeas, drained and rinsed
(optional)
½ C parsley
¼ C cilantro (optional)
2 garlic cloves
½ C water
1 lime, juiced
½ C green Chiles

INSTRUCTIONS

1. Add all the ingredients to your food processor and blend until well incorporated.

2. You may add more lime juice or hot sauce if you'd like.

CASHEW SOUR CREAM

Prep Time: 10 min | Total Time: 10 min

INGREDIENTS

1 C cashews, soaked over night
½ 1 C water
juice of one lime
1 tsp apple cider vinegar
pinch of pink salt

INSTRUCTIONS

1. Add your cashews to a high speed blender, along with everything else, blend until nice and creamy.

2. Add more water as needed to create desired consistency.

3. Refrigerate for an hour before serving to allow the cream to thicken.

SMOKEY, FEISTY FAJITAS BOWL

Prep Time: 10 min | Total Time: 40 min | Serves: 5-7 Hungry Bunnies

INGREDIENTS

1 Large red onion, sliced thin
1 red bell pepper, seeded and sliced
Cauliflower, diced small and steamed
Vegetable broth
½ tsp ground cumin
1 jalapeño pepper, seeded and diced small
3 cloves garlic, peeled and minced
¼ C chopped cilantro
2 Tbs fresh lime juice
Salt and pepper to taste
8 oz smokey tempeh, I used light life

SPICY SMOKEY KIDNEY BEANS
1 can of kidney beans
8oz green Chiles
1-2 tsp liquid smoke
salt and pepper to taste
2 Tbs hot sauce

Brown rice
Corn
Cashew nacho cheese
Kale
Pumpkin seeds

INSTRUCTIONS

1. Sauté the onion and red pepper in a skillet over high heat for 5 minutes.

2. Add vegetable broth 1 to 2 Tbs at a time to keep the vegetables from sticking to the pan.

3. Add in the smokey tempeh, seasoning, garlic, cilantro, lime juice, and salt and cook for another minute. Remove from the heat.

4. To make the spicy smokey kidney beans, add 1 can of kidney beans to a food processor along with green Chiles, liquid smoke, salt and pepper, and hot sauce. Puree until smooth and set aside.

5. Prepare your corn, nacho cheese, brown rice and serve with fresh lemon juice.

SMOKEY CHOCOLATE BBQ, SEITAN RIBS

Prep Time: 30 min | Total Time: 3 hours | Serves: 7-10 Hungry Bunnies

INGREDIENTS

DRY

2¼ C vital wheat gluten
½ C garbanzo flour
¼ C nutritional yeast

WET

1 Large red onion, sautéed
4-6 garlic cloves, sautéed
1½ C vegetable broth, for sautéing
½ C cooked chickpeas
1-¼ C Samuel Smith's organic chocolate stout, or Guinness
½ C sun-dried tomatoes, soaked to soften
3 Tbs roasted red peppers, pureed
1 Tbs chipotle peppers, in adobo sauce
½ Tbsp Worcestershire sauce
3-4 tsp liquid smoke
1 Tbs Frontier co-op Creole seasoning
3 tsp paprika
1 tsp allspice
¼ tsp pink salt
5 C BBQ sauce

Recipe adapted from Gaz Oakley

INSTRUCTIONS

1. In a blender add, sautéed onions, sautéed garlic, chickpeas, 1 C of beer, sun-dried tomatoes, roasted red peppers, chipotle peppers, Worcestershire sauce, seasonings and salt.

2. Blend to combine the mixture should be similar to a thick sauce, yet creamy. If you need to add more liquid, go ahead and add in the additional ¼ C of beer. Add the mixture to a bowl and set aside.

3. Preheat your oven to 325 F and then grab a second bowl. In that new bowl, whisk together the dry ingredients. Slowly stir in the creamy component, then begin mixing everything together with your hands.

4. Knead the mixture for about 10 minutes then form into small slabs, "racks" or "steaks" you can honestly shape them however you want, it does not matter.

5. If you would like for there to be grill marks on your slabs of seitan then go ahead and heat up a grill pan to high heat. Grill or sear the pieces about 2-3 minutes on each side or until grill marks appear.

6. Place into a Pyrex baking dish and coat with BBQ sauce. You want the pieces to be submerged, that way the flavor really soaks in. Sear the remaining pieces and continue to add them to the dish.

7. Bake for 2 hours, checking them frequently, flipping them every 30 minutes and reapplying BBQ sauce if they get dry. Allow to cool, serve with more BBQ sauce.

LEMON, CAPERS & GREEN OLIVES WITH CHIOCCIOLE

Prep Time: 20 min | Total Time: 40 min | Serves: 6-8 Hungry Bunnies

INGREDIENTS

Semolina Chiocciole pasta
1 C parsley
1 C basil
¼-½ C Cerignola olives, pitted
2-3 Tbs capers + 2 Tbs of their liquid
1 lemon juiced + zested
3-6 cloves of garlic
¼ C vegetable broth for sautéing
¼ C or a generous splash of dry white wine
1 C kale, or other dark sturdy greens, chopped small
Hemp seeds for topping
Jalapeño
Arugula

You may use whatever olives you'd like just be sure to remove their pits.

INSTRUCTIONS

1. Bring a pot of salted water to a boil water, add salt and then add the pasta. Cook according to the packaging instructions.

2. White your pasta cooks, prepare your sauce. Begin by adding parsley, basil, olives, capers + their liquid, lemon juice to a food processor. Blend until well incorporated, then transfer to a bowl and set aside.

3. Heat a large skillet on medium-high heat. Add in your garlic, season with salt and pepper and sauté until fragrant. Pour in a generous splash of white wine, about ¼ C, along with the sauce you created earlier.

4. Add in 1 C of sturdy greens and bring the sauce to a low boil, then reduce to a simmer and cover with a tight fitting lid.

5. Allow the kale to wilt but be sure to keep an eye on the amount of liquid in the pan. If you need to add more you can add some of the pasta water.

6. Drain your pasta and be sure to reserve the liquid to ensure that you have enough for your sauce, in case it needs to be thinner.

7. Add the pasta, stir everything to combine and add in the lemon zest, additional capers, fresh herbs for garnish, hemp seeds, jalapeño and arugula.

SUMMER CHILE FETTUCCINE *Mary Mirelez*

Prep Time: 20 min | Total Time: 20 min | Serves: 6-8 Hungry Bunnies

INGREDIENTS

2 packages hatch green Chile fettuccine, pastamoré brand

SALSA
1 C grape tomatoes, quartered
1 handful of cilantro + a bit more for garnish, finely, chopped
½ red onion finely, chopped
2 cans black beans, drained and rinsed
2 C roasted corn, oven roasted and cut off the cob
1 jalapeño, seeds removed and finely diced
3 limes, juiced
2 Tbs olive oil whisked together in a bowl. Add sea salt and black pepper to taste and pour over salsa. Toss to coat and store in fridge with tight fitting lid until ready to use.

PASTA SAUCE
1 C cashews
1 C filtered water
juice of 3 limes
4 cloves of garlic
½ jalapeño, seeded
pinch of cumin
pinch of sea salt and cracked black pepper

INSTRUCTIONS

1. Bring a pot of salted water to a boil water, add salt (a couple TB) and then add the pasta.

2. Stir continuously to prevent sticking. You can add olive oil if you think that works. I do, sometimes, even though science says otherwise.

3. Cook about 10 minutes or until al dente. Then proceed to make the salsa.

4. In a bowl, mix 1 C grape tomatoes, quartered, 1 handful of cilantro + a bit more for garnish, finely, chopped, ½ red onion finely, chopped, 2 cans black beans, drained and rinsed, 2 C roasted corn, oven roasted and cut off the cob, 1 jalapeño, seeds removed and finely diced.

5. Whisk together 3 limes, juiced, plus 2 Tbs of olive oil. Add Sea salt and black pepper to taste and pour over salsa. Toss to coat and store in fridge with tight fitting lid until ready to use.

6. To a blender add 1 C cashews, 1 C filtered water, juice of 3 limes, 4 cloves of garlic, ½ jalapeño seeded, pinch of cumin, pinch of sea salt and cracked black pepper. Blend until smooth and slightly heated. It'll take a few minutes.

7. Strain pasta and toss with a little olive oil. Place on serving plates or bowls. Spoon sauce over pasta and then top with salsa. Garnish with reserved cilantro.

GOCHUGARU PACCHERI WITH ROASTED RED PEPPER CREAM

Prep Time: 20 min | Total Time: 20 min | Serves: 6-8 Hungry Bunnies

INGREDIENTS

3 roasted red peppers
½ of a yellow onion, sautéed
4 cloves of garlic, sautéed
2 C soaked cashews
1 tsp gochugaru
⅔ C vegetable broth
½ C sun dried tomatoes
Paccheri pasta or pasta of choice
2-3 C sliced mushrooms, sautéed
1 Large onion, sautéed
Diced cherry tomatoes
Fresh basil

INSTRUCTIONS

1. Begin by bringing a large pot of salted water to a boil. Throw in your pasta and then begin to make your sauce.

2. To a blender, roasted red pepper, add sautéed onion, sautéed garlic, soaked cashews, gochugaru chili, vegetable broth and sun dried tomatoes. Blend on high until smooth and creamy.

3. Once the pasta is finished cooking, drain it and be sure to reserve some of the pasta water.

4. Pour the sauce over the pasta, if you want the sauce to be thinner add some of the pasta water, use as little or as much of it as you'd like.

5. Serve with sautéed mushrooms and onions, diced cherry tomatoes and fresh basil.

ASPARAGUS + MUSHROOM RISOTTO *Magdalena Nickl*

Prep Time: 40 min | Total Time: 70 min | Serves: 3 Hungry Bunnies

INGREDIENTS

1⅔ C risotto rice
5¼ C vegetable broth
1 tsp apple cider vinegar
17-18 oz mushrooms
17-18 oz asparagus
1 tsp tahini
2 tsp soy sauce
2 Tbs oat milk
½ tsp garlic powder
salt and pepper to taste
½ tsp paprika powder
1 tsp sugar
1 heaping teaspoon corn starch
1 Tbs vegetable oil

INSTRUCTIONS

1. Add risotto rice to a large pot along with broth and apple cider vinegar. After the water is boiling turn the temperature down to low heat and let it simmer for about 25 minutes. Stir your risotto rice every 5-10 minutes to make sure that it doesn't burn into the pot.

2. In the meantime wash and cut off the ends of your asparagus and cut it into bite-sized pieces. Preheat a pan and add the asparagus along with 1 Tbs oil and some salt and pepper to the pan. Let this sit for 10-15 minutes on medium heat.

3. In another pan prepare mushrooms. Cut them into thin slices and add them along with garlic powder, paprika, salt and pepper, sugar, oil and 1 tsp soy sauce to the pan.

4. While the veggies are cooking we have time to make a delicious sauce. Grab a pot and bring 1 C of vegetable stock to a boil.

5. Now add 1 tsp soy sauce, 1 tsp tahini, oat milk and some garlic powder. Combine corn starch with a little bit of water in separate a bowl and add this to your sauce.

6. Now immediately start to whisk everything around and turn down the temperature to low heat. When your asparagus is nice and tender, add 3 Tbs of the sauce to it and let this sit for another 2 minutes.

7. Combine the risotto rice, the asparagus, the mushrooms and another 3 tablespoons of the sauce. Enjoy!

SUN DRIED TOMATO PASTE, PESTO, ARUGULA & LEMON PIZZA

Prep Time: 10 min | Total Time: 40 min | Serves: 5-7 Hungry Bunnies

INGREDIENTS

Whole grain pizza dough
Pesto
Sun dried tomato paste
Arugula
Lemon
Follow your heart smoked Gouda cheese

INSTRUCTIONS

1. For this recipe I used store bought dough, you can get some at any local pizzeria or at whole foods at the pizza counter.

2. Place a rack in the lower third of the oven and preheat to 525 F. or as high as oven will go.

3. Open the packaging for your dough and place it on an oiled baking sheet. Allow the dough to puff up a bit in a warm place.

4. Once dough has risen in baking sheet, top with all the toppings and whatever else you'd like to add.

5. Bake until golden brown and crisp on bottom and sides, 20–30 minutes. Top with arugula and squeeze on fresh lemon juice to serve.

HARISSA ROASTED EGGPLANT

Prep Time: 5 min | Total Time: 50 min | Serves: 3-5 Hungry Bunnies

INGREDIENTS

2 (1-lb.) Eggplants, halved lengthwise
¼ C olive oil
¼ C harissa sauce
1 tsp pink salt
¼ tsp black pepper

INSTRUCTIONS

1. Score the flesh side of each eggplant half in a cross-hatch pattern. Be careful not to cut through the skin.

2. Place eggplant halves on a silpat lined baking sheet.

3. Brush oil evenly over flesh side of eggplant halves then spoon on and spread out the harissa.

4. Bake at 400 F. for 40 to 45 minutes.

5. Season with salt and pepper and serve with tahini drizzled over top.

BUTTER CHICKEN *Marie-Kristin Wasler*

Prep Time: 5 min | Total Time: 50 min | Serves: 3-5 Hungry Bunnies

INGREDIENTS

8 cloves garlic, minced
1 dried bay leaf
1 Tbsp cumin seeds
1 Tbsp coriander seeds
300g tomatoes
½ C cashews
1 can coconut milk
1 big red onion, roughly chopped
250g smoked tofu, cut into small cubes
½ Tbsp garam masala
3 Tbsp authentic curry powder
Cayenne pepper
Salt
Pepper

INSTRUCTIONS

1. On medium heat, sauté cumin seeds, coriander seeds and bay leaf with vegetable oil. Add minced garlic and sauté for 2 more minutes.

2. Add tomatoes and cashews and sauté until the tomatoes fall apart and form a sauce. Add water if needed.

3. Add everything to a blender, add coconut milk and blend until creamy.

4. In the meantime, sauté smoked tofu and onion with garam masala.

5. Add the mixed tomato sauce to the tofu, add curry powder and cook about 20 minutes.

6. Add salt, pepper and cayenne pepper to taste.

7. Top with fresh coriander or parsley, lime juice, toasted cashews (optional) and serve with rice.

ROASTED, COMFORT BOWL WITH DICED TOMATOES

Prep Time: 15 min | Total Time: 50 min | Serves: 3-5 Hungry Bunnies

INGREDIENTS

Peppers, onions and potatoes
½ white onion, sautéed
4-6 cloves of garlic, sautéed
1 C veggie broth
1 Tbs Italian seasoning
28 oz can of crushed tomatoes
1 kg Jackfruit, in brine, rinsed and drained
Romaine
Tahini lemon vinaigrette
Sauerkraut kimchi, I use the brand Eden
Brown rice

INSTRUCTIONS

1. In a large heated skillet, sauté onions and garlic in vegetable broth. Add in seasoning as well as the can of crushed tomatoes and the 1 kg or 4-5 C of rinsed & drained jackfruit.

2. Allow the mixture to come to a boil then reduce to a simmer & cook for roughly 20-30 minutes.

3. Prepare your peppers, onions and potatoes. I use the recipe for my peppers, onions and potatoes sandwich and I simply use sweet potatoes instead of regular ones.

4. Check on the jackfruit mixture, taste and adjust seasoning according to preference.

5. Serve everything in a bowl with brown rice, sauerkraut kimchi and tahini lemon vinaigrette.

SPINACH & ARTICHOKE STROMBOLI

Prep Time: 20 min | Total Time: 30 min | Serves: 8-10 Hungry Bunnies

INGREDIENTS

Whole grain pizza dough
2 Tbs vegetable broth
3 large cloves garlic, diced small
2 C marinated artichoke hearts, chopped
5-6 C baby spinach diced
Violife 'Just Like Parmesan' Wedge
¼-½ C dry white wine
salt and pepper to taste

INSTRUCTIONS

1. Preheat oven to 400 F. Heat your vegetable broth in a pan over medium heat.

2. Add garlic and sauté for 1 minute, stirring frequently. Add artichoke hearts, white wine and spinach and sauté until spinach is wilted. Let the liquid cook out as much as possible, it would be better for it to cook out rather then have to drain it and lose all those flavors. Transfer to a bowl and set to the side.

3. Open the packaging for your dough and place it on an oiled baking sheet, or on a silpat mat for an oil free recipe. Allow the dough to puff up a bit in a warm place.

4. Once dough has risen in baking sheet, add the spinach and artichoke filling and grate on some of the Violife 'Just Like Parmesan' Wedge. You can use as little or as much of this as you'd like.

5. Bake until golden brown and crisp on bottom and sides, 20–30 minutes.

SMOKEY BBQ BUDDHA BOWL

Prep Time: 20 min | Total Time: 30 min | Serves: 8-10 Hungry Bunnies

INGREDIENTS

BBQ cauliflower bites
Oven roasted potatoes
with BBQ seasoning

SMOKEY MARINATED BBQ TEMPEH
8 oz smokey tempeh, I used light life
Homemade BBQ sauce

Red cabbage sauerkraut, to serve
Steamed corn

INSTRUCTIONS

1. Begin by preparing your oven roasted potatoes with BBQ seasoning as well as BBQ cauliflower bites.

2. For the smokey marinated tempeh you are going to want to marinade everything the night before. Add the tempeh to a container and cover them with BBQ sauce. You want them to be completely submerged in sauce.

3. Once the tempeh has marinated, transfer it, as well as the BBQ sauce it soaked in, to a skillet and bring to a boil.

4. Reduce the tempeh to a simmer and let it cook for 10-15 minutes.

5. Serve everything together with some steamed corn and red cabbage sauerkraut.

CAULIFLOWER CARBONARA

Prep Time: 10 min | Total Time: 30 min | Serves: 6-8 Hungry Bunnies

INGREDIENTS

1 Tbs olive oil
1 Large onion, sautéed
2 Tbs garlic, minced, sautéed
1 C creamy cauliflower sauce
pasta of choice
1 C peas, steamed
½ C parsley, minced
6 Tbs nutritional yeast
1 Tbs bread crumbs
Pink salt and pepper to taste
Oven roasted cherry tomatoes

INSTRUCTIONS

1. Heat up a large skillet and sauté your onions and garlic. Set aside.

2. Bring a large pot of salted water to a boil and add in your pasta. Once the pasta is finished cooking, drain it and reserve some of the pasta water.

3. Mix in the creamy cauliflower sauce, steamed peas, parsley, nutritional yeast, oven roasted tomatoes, bread crumbs, salt and pepper.

CREAMY CAULIFLOWER SAUCE

Prep Time: 10 min | Total Time: 10 min

INGREDIENTS

2 C steamed cauliflower
2¼ C vegetable broth
½ C olive oil
salt and pepper to taste

INSTRUCTIONS

1. Add your everything to your high speed blender and puree until smooth.

TALLARINES VERDES *Tawnya Brown*

Prep Time: 15 min | Total Time: 15 min

INGREDIENTS

1 handful of fresh basil

1 bag or bunch of spinach

2 C unsweetened almond milk

¼ C pine nuts

3 Tbs nutritional yeast

¼ C vegan mozzarella

½ onion, sautéed in olive oil

4 cloves of garlic, minced and sautéed

salt and pepper too taste

*Pine nuts are expensive, so a good substitute is sunflower seeds.

INSTRUCTIONS

1. Add all ingredients to your blender, blend on high.

2. Prepare your pasta according to packaging instructions.

3. Pour your sauce over top and serve.

CAPONATA *Michelle Gerrard-Marriott*

Prep Time: 30 min | Total Time: 30 min

INGREDIENTS

Extra Virgin Olive Oil
2 large Eggplants , cut into fairly large pieces
2 tsp fresh minced oregano
1 small red onion chopped
4-5 cloves garlic , peeled and finely minced
1 small bunch fresh flat-leaf parsley , leaves picked and stalks minced
Handful of basil ribboned
2 mint leaves minced
3 Tbs capers
1 handful green olives roughly chopped and de-pitted
2-3 Tbs herbed vinegar made with fig balsamic
5 large ripe tomatoes, roughly chopped
2 Tbs toasted slivered almonds
Pink salt + Pepper to Taste

INSTRUCTIONS

1. First place your fig balsamic in a small bowl and add minced basil, parsley, oregano and a touch of mint.

2. Coat a large cast iron pan in olive oil and place on a medium high heat. Add your eggplant and oregano with a bit of salt and pepper and gently mix to combine.

3. Make sure the eggplant is evenly coated in the oil. Dance around your kitchen and cook for about 6-8 minutes, gently stirring the pan every 2 minutes. You want the eggplant to reach a gorgeous golden color.

4. Once you get that color add your onion, garlic, parsley stalks and a couple minced leaves and continue to cook until fragrant.

5. Toss in your capers and olives then drizzle over your herb fig balsamic. Allow to thicken and then add your tomatoes and simmer for 20 minutes until the aroma fills your home and the eggplant and tomatoes are tender.

6. Season with pink salt and pepper to taste. Feel free to add in some red chili flakes for a kick and serve with another drizzle of olive oil, vinegar, parsley and your toasted almonds! Enjoy.

Photography by her beautiful friend Andrew Mangiona

CREAMY BROCCOLI PASTA *Sam Pickthall*

Prep Time: 15 min | Total Time: 40 min | Serves: 4-3 Hungry Bunnies

INGREDIENTS

PASTA
1 x 400g packet spiral pasta, gluten free if preferred

BROCCOLI MIXTURE
1 Tbsp coconut oil
1 large stalk leek, trimmed and thinly sliced
2 cloves garlic, peeled and minced
1 medium-large head broccoli, cut into florets
Pinch of pink salt

WHITE SAUCE
60g coconut oil
2 cloves garlic, peeled and minced
7 Tbsp gluten free all purpose flour, I use 'Bob's Red Mill Gluten Free 1:1 Baking Flour'
3 cups almond milk or plant-based milk of choice
½ tsp ground nutmeg
1 tsp pink salt
1 tsp cracked black pepper
1 Tbsp nutritional yeast
1 stalk spring onion, thinly sliced, to garnish

INSTRUCTIONS

1. Cook pasta according to packet instructions. Scoop out 1 C of the cooking water and set aside. Drain off water and set pasta aside until ready.

2. Melt oil over a medium-high heat in a large pot, Add sliced leek and sauté for 2 minutes to soften. Stir through minced garlic and sauté for a further 3-4 minutes or until leek is soft and slightly translucent. Add in broccoli florets, pinch of salt and mix well with the leek for 2-3 minutes or until broccoli begins to cook through.

4. Reduce heat to medium-low and cover pot with a lid. Let broccoli steam in the pot for 3-4 minutes or until tender, stirring occasionally. Whilst broccoli is cooking, make the white sauce.

5. Melt oil in a medium size saucepan over medium heat, add minced garlic and cook for 1 minute until fragrant. Stir in flour, cooking gently for 1 minute with a whisk.

6. Gradually pour in milk, whisking until thickened and small bubbles begin to appear on the surface, don't boil.

Reduce heat to low and add in nutmeg, salt, pepper and nutritional yeast, whisk well. Turn off heat, set aside.

7. Once broccoli is soft and tender, stir through cooked pasta.

8. Carefully pour the white sauce over the broccoli pasta, followed by the reserved 1 cup of cooking pasta water. Gently mix pasta to combine well with the sauce.

GRILLED EGGPLANT PIZZA HEIRLOOM TOMATO + PESTO & LIME CHILI SAUCE

Prep Time: 10 min | Total Time: 40 min | Serves: 5-7 Hungry Bunnies

INGREDIENTS

Whole grain pizza dough
Pesto
Grilled eggplant
Miyokos mozzarella
Heirloom tomato
Basil
Lime chili sauce
Red onion

INSTRUCTIONS

1. For this recipe I used store bought dough, you can get some at any local pizzeria or at whole foods at the pizza counter.

2. Place a rack in the lower third of the oven and preheat to 525 F. or as high as oven will go.

3. Open the packaging for your dough and place it on an oiled baking sheet. Allow the dough to puff up a bit in a warm place.

4. Once dough has risen in baking sheet, top with all the toppings and whatever else you'd like to add.

5. Bake until golden brown and crisp on bottom and sides, 20–30 minutes. Top with lime chili sauce and fresh basil.

DEVOUR

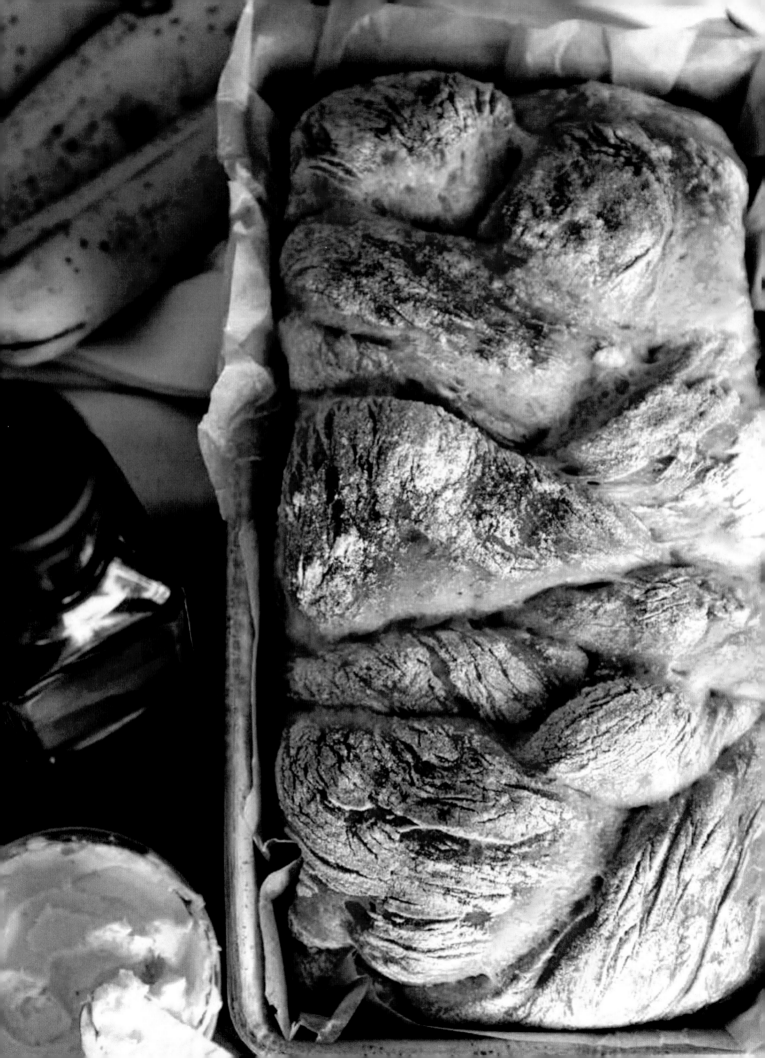

BRAIDED SPELT BRIOCHE CHALLAH BREAD

Prep Time: 3 hours | Total Time: 3 hours 30 min

INGREDIENTS

1 C water, warm not hot

1 Tbs coconut sugar

1 Tbs active dry yeast

¼ C olive oil

1 medium banana, mashed not pureed

3½ C spelt flour

additional spelt flour as needed

*If you do not have a electric mixer, you can knead the dough by hand about 10 minutes.

**Recipe adapted and inspired by Melissa, The Balanced Blueberry

INSTRUCTIONS

1. Mix the coconut sugar and yeast into the water to dissolve. Let this sit for 5 minutes, the mixture will puff up a bit.

2. In a separate bowl, mix olive oil, and mashed banana very well.

3. Using a stand mixer with the dough hook, combine yeast mixture, banana mixture, and the flour.

4. Gradually add more as needed, 1 C at a time, then knead for 5 minutes. You want the dough to be gummy but smooth.

5. The dough should be smooth and should not stick to your hands. Then transfer to a well oiled bowl and cover with a damp towel in a warm place for one hour.

6. Once the dough doubles in size remove it from the bowl and begin to form your brioche. Divide the dough into three equal sections, then on a floured board, roll each portion into a long log. If at any point you feel the dough becomes warm and sticky, chill it in the fridge for at least ten minutes.

7. Braid the three portions like you would braid hair with equal space between the knots. Let the brioche rise for another 10-20 minutes.

8. Bake at 350 F. for 30 minutes until the surface is lightly golden and a temperature registers 200 F. Do not over bake.

9. Allow to cool completely before serving and serve with truffle butter.

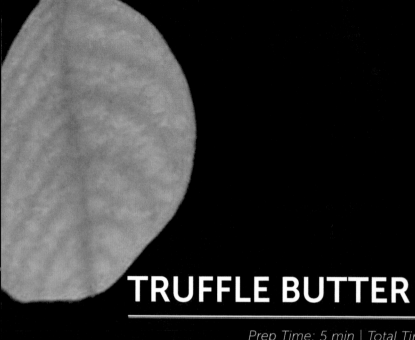

TRUFFLE BUTTER

Prep Time: 5 min | Total Time: 5 min

INGREDIENTS

1 pack of Miyokos butter, softened
2-3 Tbs truffle oil

INSTRUCTIONS

1. Whip the butter and the oil together using an electric mixer. Chill before serving.

CINNAMON SUGAR BUTTER

Prep Time: 5 min | Total Time: 5 min

INGREDIENTS

½ C Miyokos butter, softened
½ tsp vanilla extract
1 tsp cinnamon
3-4 Tbs coconut sugar

INSTRUCTIONS

1. Add all of your ingredients to a bowl, whisk until smooth and creamy. Chill before serving.

CHOCOLATE HAZELNUT BUTTER CAKE

Prep Time: 3 hours | Total Time: 3 hours 30 min

INGREDIENTS

2 C Self rising flour + 1 C for adjustments

¼ tsp pink Himalayan salt

2 tsp baking soda

1 tsp baking powder

¼-½ C coconut sugar

1 C unsweetened cacao powder

2 C Almond milk

2 tsp apple cider vinegar

½ C unsweetened apple sauce

½ C hazelnut butter

½-1 C of Enjoy Life Foods chocolate chips

PEANUT BUTTER VANILLA ICING

1-2 Cans of Coconut Cream, refrigerated overnight

1 vanilla bean

3 Heaping Tbs of PB2 powder

* You may use 1 C almond milk 1 C water instead of 2 C of almond milk

INSTRUCTIONS

1. Preheat the oven to 350 F & lightly spray olive oil into your cake pan.

2. Add 2 C of the self rising flour, pink Himalayan salt, baking soda, baking powder, coconut sugar, unsweetened cacao powder to your food processor. Pulse until combined. If you don't have a food processor then add these ingredients to a mixing bowl & whisk them together.

3. Begin to add the wet ingredients. Add in the apple cider vinegar, olive oil, & hazelnut extract. Pulse the mixture about 2 times, do not blend just pulse. If you are using bowls then go ahead & carefully add these ingredients in and fold the batter.

4. Now you can slowly add the nut milk. This is important, you may not need the 3rd & final cup of flour if the batter begins to form & be creamy & smooth. Generally I add & adjust both flour & nut milk at this point (in small portions) in order to make sure the batter is not too thin or not too thick & clumpy.

5. Taste the batter & adjust sweetness if needed, I personally do not like a very sweet cake so you may want to add more sugar to your liking. You may also add your chocolate chips if you are planning to add them.

PINEAPPLE COCONUT
CHIA POPSICLES *Christina Kee*

Prep Time: 10 min | Total Time: 60 min

INGREDIENTS

1 can full fat coconut milk
2 Tbs chia seeds
1½ tsp vanilla extract
1 Tbs maple syrup
3 C chopped pineapple chunks
½ Fresh lime

INSTRUCTIONS

1. In bowl mix coconut milk, chia seeds, vanilla extract, and maple syrup.

2. Let set in the fridge for chia seeds to set for approximately 50 minutes.

3. For layered effect, pour into Popsicle molds and place in freezer until partially frozen.

4. While this freezes, blend pineapple and juice of ½ a fresh lime in the blender.

5. Pour over the frozen coconut layer, and continue to freeze until ready.

LUNA CAKES

Prep Time: 5 min | Total Time: 15 min | Serves: 5-7 Hungry Bunnies

INGREDIENTS

1 C semolina flour
½ C tapioca starch
1 C water
⅓ tsp adobo
Recipe adapted from Elavegan

INSTRUCTIONS

1. Add all of your ingredients to your food processor and blend until the batter is smooth. Add 1 C of water.

2. Add some of the batter into a non-stick pan

3. For layered effect, pour into Popsicle molds and place in freezer until partially frozen.

4. Cook them similar to pancakes, when small bubbles form, flip them.

WHITE CHOCOLATE CUPCAKES *Jean Charite*

Prep Time: 15 min | Total Time: 40 min

INGREDIENTS

2 C organic all purpose flour
1 tsp baking powder
½ C raw cane sugar
1 C unsweetened almond milk
1 tsp vanilla extract
2 egg (EnerG Egg Replacer) serving
½ C Raw Cocoa Butter Oil (3 oz Health works Organic Raw Cacao Butter)
Pinch of Himalayan Salt

INSTRUCTIONS

1. Place Raw Cocoa in a sauce pan and allow to melt under allow heat.

2. Once the cacao has fully melted, remove from heat and allow the now oil to cool to room temp. (A slight skin will develop but that's fine.)

3. Mix egg replacer (follow instructions for 2 eggs) and allow the mix to sit at room temperature for at least 10 minutes.

4. Set out ½ C of vegan margin (buttery sticks) and allow it to soften. I like to place it on the stove while the oven preheats Preheat over for 350 F.

5. In a mixing bowl, add flour, baking powder, cane sugar, salt and mix well. Pour in milk, then egg replacer mix, then cacao oil into mixing bowl and continue to stir until you get a nice smooth cake batter

6. If batter appears to be too thick, thin it out by adding more milk 1-2 tbsp at a time.

7. Place your desired cake cups in a cup cake mold and fill each cut with the cake mix ¾ fill from the top

8. Place the mold in the preheated oven and allow the cupcakes to bake for 25-30 minutes.

9. The cupcakes will not go full brown, ensure that hey are fully baked by inserting a toothpick they the center of the cupcakes. Tooth pick should pull out with "dry" (without cake mix)

RASPBERRY BUTTER CREAM ICING *Jean Charite*

Prep Time: 15 min | Total Time: 40 min

INGREDIENTS

1 C of raspberries
2 Tbs raw cane sugar
4-5 C organic powdered sugar
½ C Earth Balance Buttery Sticks (1 stick)

INSTRUCTIONS

1. You can use either fresh or frozen raspberries for this icing. Ambient temps may affect the consistency of your icing. Be mindful of the season as well as the current temperature of your cooking area. You may need to increase or decrease ingredients to compensate.

2. Add raspberries to sauce pan and allow them to simmer over low medium heat while crushing them.

3. Remove from heat then pass the berries through a sieve to achieve a raspberry purée leaving the seeds behind.

4. In a mixing bowl at your softened margin, powdered sugar, and cane sugar and combine using a whisk or electric mixer.

5. Add the raspberry purée into the mix and continue to stir. If the batter is too thick add water (1-2tbsp at a time) to thin it out. If the batter is to thin add more powdered sugar (¼ cup at a time) to thicken.

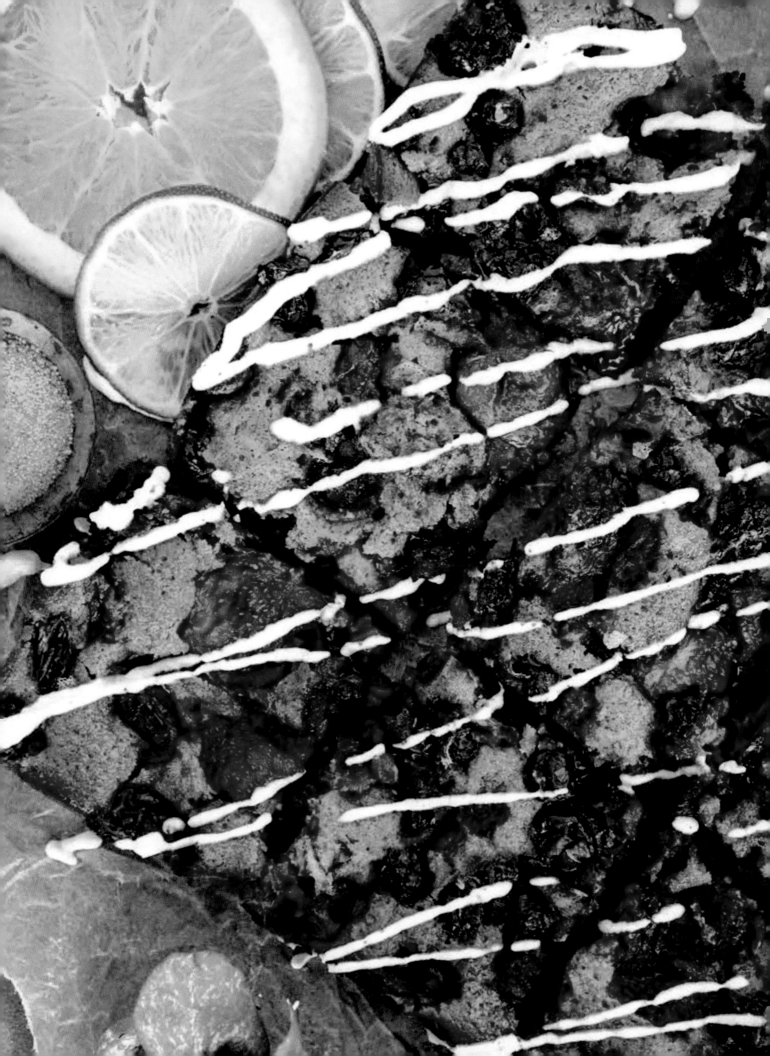

SUMMER BERRY COBBLER

Prep Time: 15 min | Total Time: 1 hour 15 min | Serves: 5 Hungry Bunnies

INGREDIENTS

¼ C + 2 Tbs olive oil
¼-½ C + 2 Tbs sugar
1 C self-rising flour
1 C almond milk
2 C fresh (or frozen) mixed berries

INSTRUCTIONS

1. Preheat the oven to 350 F. Apply olive oil to a 3 quart baking.

2. In a bowl, mix the sugar, flour and milk, then add the olive oil.

3. Pour the batter into the baking dish then add the mixed berries over top.

4. Sprinkle some coconut sugar over the berries and then place in the oven and bake for 1 hour or until golden brown and bubbly.

5. Serve with coconut whipped cream.

SWEET CASHEW CREAM

Prep Time: 5 min | Total Time: 5 min | Serves: 10-13 Hungry Bunnies

INGREDIENTS

2 C cashews
2 C water
¼ C maple syrup
¼ tsp pink salt
1 vanilla bean

INSTRUCTIONS

1. Add all ingredients into your Vitamix or high-speed blender and blend until thick and creamy.

GOOEY ZUCCHINI
BROWNIES *Marie-Kristin Wasler*

Prep Time: 15 min | Total Time: 45 min

INGREDIENTS

1 C grated zucchini
¾ C peanut butter
¼ C maple syrup
¼ C cocoa powder
2 Tbsp flax seeds
2 Tbsp hemp hearts
¾ Tbsp baking soda
¼ C chocolate chips
Pinch of pink salt

INSTRUCTIONS

1. Preheat the oven to 350 F grease a baking tin with coconut oil.

2. Put all ingredients in a bowl and mix until combined.

3. Transfer the mixture into the baking tin and pat it down with wet hands. If desired, sprinkle with more chocolate chips.

4. Bake for 30 minutes. Let it cool down and then transfer the baked brownies into your fridge for at least one hour.

5. Serve with coconut whipped cream.

TARALLI DOLCE DI PASQUA

Prep Time: 15 min | Total Time: 40 min

INGREDIENTS

4½ C all-purpose flour
1 tsp baking powder
1 tsp baking soda
¾ C olive oil
1 C+ ¾ C coconut sugar
3 flax eggs
¼-½ C anisette
1½ C raw cashews, soaked
½ C water +¼ C if needed
juice of 1 large lemon
1 tsp lemon zest
dash of onion powder
Himalayan sea salt & cracked pepper, to taste

CITRUS SUGAR GLAZE
Powdered sugar
Lemon juice, orange juice
Anise extract
Turmeric
Recipe adapted form Hot for Food

INSTRUCTIONS

1. Begin by preheating your oven to 350 F. In a large bowl combine flour with baking powder and baking soda and set aside. Mix your flax egg and let it thicken for 10 minutes. 1 tbsp flax+3 tbsp water=1 egg.

2. In a vitamin blender, blend 1½ C raw cashews, ½ C water+¼C if needed, juice of 1 large lemon (1 Tbs) + 1 tsp lemon zest, dash of onion powder, pink Himalayan sea salt & cracked pepper, to taste. Blend on high until smooth and creamy, set aside.

3. In stand mixer, blend the olive oil with the coconut sugar. Add the anisette and flax egg while the mixer is still running. Add the cashew mixture to your 'wet' ingredients, this is a replacement for the ricotta cheese.

4. Gradually add the flour mixture 1 C at a time and fold it into the batter until you have a soft ball of dough. Taste and adjust to see if you would like to add more anisette.

5. Line your baking sheet with a silpat baking mat or with parchment paper. Using a Tbs, scoop out balls of the tough, you may leave them round which is how they are traditionally made but I preferred to braid them. Do not flatten them! Bake for 12-17 minutes.

6. Allow cookies to cool completely before icing. In the meantime sift vegan confectionery sugar into a bowl and slowly add orange juice and lemon juice. I eyeballed it, you may add ½ tsp of anise extract to this. Drizzle the cooled cookies.

MATCHA TIRAMISU WITH VANILLA WHISKEY CREAM

Prep Time: 15 min | Total Time: 40 min

INGREDIENTS

SPONGE CAKE
1¼ C all-purpose flour
½ tsp pink salt
2-3 tsp matcha
¾ C coconut sugar (to your liking)
1 tsp baking soda
1 tsp baking powder
⅔ C non-dairy milk (such as soy or almond)
⅓ C olive oil
2 Tbs apple cider vinegar
1 vanilla bean

MATCHA CREAM
1½ C cashews, soaked overnight
¼ tsp pink salt
¾ C of Matcha green tea
¼ C coconut nectar
2 tsp olive oil

VANILLA WHISKEY CREAM
1½ C cashews
¼ tsp pink salt
¼ C coconut nectar
1 vanilla bean
1 Tbs whiskey

MATCHA SOAKING SYRUP
¾ C hot water
2 tsp matcha powder
3 Tbs coconut sugar
1 Tbsp whiskey, optional

INSTRUCTIONS

1. Preheat your oven to 350 F. Prepare a small 8x8 baking pan by spraying with a bit of coconut oil. For the Sponge add your dry ingredients to a bowl and mix to incorporate. In a separate bowl whisk together your wet ingredients, then carefully add the wet to the dry.

2. Be sure to mix everything well, but you do not want to over mix. Pour the mixture into your 8x8 tin and bake at 350 F. for 12-16 minutes. Keep an eye on the cake to ensure it does not overcook and become dry. When they are finished a toothpick, or knife should come out clean. Then move on to make your Vanilla Cream.

3. Add the ingredients for the Vanilla Cream. Blend until smooth, then place in a bowl and set aside.

4. For your Matcha Cream, add all of the ingredients to your blender and blend on high until smooth. If the mixture is too thick for your liking, you may add plant milk 1/4 C at a time. When finished blending pour into a bowl and set to the side. Whisk together the ingredients for the Matcha soaking syrup in a bowl and set aside so you can check on your sponge cake.

5. Allow the sponge cake to cool completely, then you may begin layering your mini tiramisu's! I used small mason jars.

CITRUS & ROSEMARY COBBLER

Prep Time: 15 min | Total Time: 1 hour 15 min | Serves: 5 Hungry Bunnies

INGREDIENTS

¼ C + 2 Tbs olive oil
¼-½ C + 2 Tbs sugar
1 C self-rising flour
2 Tbs lemon zest
1 Tbs lemon extract
1 C almond milk
lemon slices for decoration
1 Tbs finely chopped fresh rosemary

INSTRUCTIONS

1. Preheat the oven to 350 F. Apply olive oil to a 3 quart baking.

2. In a bowl, mix the sugar, lemon zest, lemon extract, flour and milk, 1 Tbs finely chopped fresh rosemary, then add the oil.

3. Pour the batter into the baking dish then place the lemon slices over top, this is optional and is purely for looks.

4. Sprinkle some coconut sugar over the top and then place in the oven and bake for 1 hour or until golden brown and bubbly.

5. Serve with coconut whipped cream or sweet cashew cream.

CORNY CORNBREAD

Prep Time: 15 min | Total Time: 45 min | Serves: 7 Hungry Bunnies

INGREDIENTS

ALMOND BUTTERMILK
1 C + 3 Tbsp plain unsweetened almond
milk + 1 tsp apple cider vinegar

1 tsp baking soda
4 flax egg
1-1½ C steamed corn
¼ C + 2 Tbs
¼ C coconut sugar
4 Tbsp unsweetened applesauce
1 C + 3 Tbsp fine yellow cornmeal
1 C + 3 Tbsp spelt flour
¼ tsp pink salt
¼ tsp black pepper

INSTRUCTIONS

1. Preheat oven to 350 F. and prepare a
muffin tin.

2. Make your flax egg and set it aside for
a few minutes. Mix almond milk and the
apple cider vinegar, allow it to curdle for a
few minutes, stir in the baking soda and set
to the side.

3. In a separate bowl, add your oil and
sugar. Begin to whisk the two, then add the
unsweetened applesauce, flax egg, and mix
again. Add the almond buttermilk mixture
and mix once more.

4. Add pink salt, pepper, cornmeal, and
spelt flour and stir once or twice, just to
incorporate. You want the mixture to be
thin and lumpy. Add the corn and gently
fold it in.

5. Bake for 30-35 minutes or until the edges
are golden brown. Serve warm, with butter.

BAKED VEGAN CHEESECAKE *Rebecca Doudak*

Prep Time: 5 min | Total Time: 1 hour | Serves: 5-7 Hungry Bunnies

INGREDIENTS

18 Belvita cookies
3 Tbs butter
1½ C raw cashews
⅔ C chickpeas
1 lemon zest
½ lemon, juiced
2 Tbs vanilla extract
1 Tbs 1 tsp arrowroot flour
⅓ C agave
1 Tbs 1 tsp tahini
1 C full fat coconut milk
¼ tsp salt
2 Tbs apple cider vinegar
6 inch spring form pan
parchment paper

BLUEBERRY TOPPING

2 C of blueberries
2 Tbs of lemon juice
¼ C coconut sugar
2 Tbs cornstarch
3 Tbs of water

INSTRUCTIONS

1. Coat spring form pan with a thin layer of butter then line with parchment paper.

2. Use one circle piece at the bottom and one strip around the sides. Process Belvita cookies and butter until a crumbly crust is formed.

3. Press crust into the bottom of the spring form pan and slightly up the sides. Refrigerate while you're preparing everything else.

4. Boil water and soak cashews for 15 minutes. Combine drained cashews and everything else in a blender and blend till creamy.

5. Pour filling on crust. Bake at 350° for 45 minutes. Let cool at room temperature for one hour and then refrigerate for at least three hours.

6. Heat 2 C of blueberries, 2 Tbs of lemon juice ¼ C coconut sugar and a splash of water in a small sauce pan until it simmers.

7. Add in 2 Tbs of cornstarch dissolved in 3 Tbs of water. Simmer the topping on low until thickened.

RECIPE INDEX